what people are saying about

21st CENTURY
SUPERHUMAN

Coming from a hungry generation of seekers, with innate sparks of desire for truth and awakening, I can say that **21st Century Superhuman** *is truly a powerful tool and masterpiece. A collection of wisdom, encouragement, information, and history. This book is a game changer. Information you may have already have is worded better then ever before, hitting home and resonating with you on every page. New essential information for the collective is presented, yet feels familiar to the soul.* **21st Century Superhuman** *is a great treasure for every home.*

Amber JoAnn Cook
Young Mom, Bright Light

The book **21st Century Super Human** *will be a huge key for the shift into multi-dimensional transformation and ascension of the individual, as well as for the Planet as a whole. As we move into living from the Heart and growing towards reaching our full potential,* **21st Century Superhuman** *gives you a jump-start into the process. No matter what age you are, young or old, or what point of the path you are on, this book needs to be on your shelf.*

Sam V. Meyering
Food Magician, Energy Worker

Love your book! There was only one copy left at the workshop and I got it! My friend borrowed it, and I can't wait to get it back! She is going to buy her own copy, yay!

So grateful you put this kind of a guidebook together. It contains so many far reaching correlations with the cutting edge, mindful teachings of so many respected others, Dr. Michael Ryce included. Truly a book who's time has come. My friend and I are considering using it as the "Master" text to teach a class.

Your book is a "strong spiritual backbone," covering the fact and the potential that now, there are really so many brain cells already in place in people's minds, ripe for further cultivation.... (Yay!) This is what we are teaching:

"Are we declaring, and faithfully applying what We Know fearlessly, and powerfully? Are we actualizing our True Design LOVE Now? YES!"

Julie Matthews
Piano Instructor, Quantum Mentor

21st CENTURY SUPERHUMAN
Quantum Lifestyle

Live Your Potential NOW!

Part 4
BODY

Rejuvenation and Growing Younger with Healthy Eating, Cleanse & Detox

by Cary Ellis, DD
with Theodora Mulder, PhD
Front Cover Art by Franzi Talley

ALSO BY: Cary Ellis
Super Immunity Secrets -Fifty Vegan-Vegetarian Recipes & Immune Protective Herbs
Why Become a Vegetarian?
Benefits for Health and Longevity; Truth About Weight Loss

21st Century Superhuman
Protectrite Copyright 2013 © by Cary Ellis
ISBN-10: 0-9841711-8-5 (Virtual Earth Village Publishing)
ISBN-13: 978-0-9841711-8-7 (Virtual Earth Village Publishing)

DISCLAIMER

The authors of this book do not dispense medical advice or prescribe the use of any technique as a form of treatment for physical, mental, emotional or medical issues or problems without the advice of a physician, either directly or indirectly. The intent of the authors and publisher, is to offer information of a general nature to help you in your quest for emotional and spiritual well-being. In the event you use any of the information in this book for yourself, which is your right, the authors and the publisher assume no responsibility for your actions. References are provided for informational purposes only and do not constitute endorsement of any websites or other sources. Readers should be aware that the websites listed in this book may change. We wish you well in your journey!

VirtualEarthVillage.com

Virtual Earth Village Publishing
http://www.virtualearthvillage.com

To our Sisters and Brothers on
Planet Earth:

May We Live in a Way that
Aligns with our Greatest Potential,
Fortified by Nature's simple Wisdom
Grounded in Deep LOVE,
Compassion and Gratitude
Inspired to Infinite Possibilities.

And may we offer,
There is only one time
when it is essential to Awaken...

~ THAT TIME IS NOW ~

READING: 21st Century Superhuman

Expand Your Brain-Power

Bold, italics, hyphens, commas, caps out of the ordinary suggest rich New meanings. When you bump into them, boldly expand use of your Mind into compelling New territories. Our explanation of Quantum physics is easy enough for a six year old to understand (as Einstein says), and it shifts us into tantalizing freedom of Mind-Body-Spirit that transcends limiting superstitions of former generations. Specially denoted words, phrasing and punctuation skyrocket understanding, to catch current waves of miraculous acceleration.

A mind stretched by new experience
can never go back to its old dimensions.

Oliver Wendell Holmes (1809-1894)
Progressive Physician, Author

Shift of the Ages, Shift
Field of Possibilities, Cloud of Possibilities, Field of Consciousness, Field, Divine Matrix, Web of Life, Plenum, Vacuum
Essence, Effluvia
Conversational comments from Author and Contributor in italics
21st Century Superhumans, 21st Century Superhuman, Quantum Lifestyle,
Arc the Hologram, Arcing the Hologram
Yeshua-Jesus,
Mirror, Mirrored, Mirroring, Mind-Heart
LOVE, Not of LOVE, True Design LOVE, True Infinite Design LOVE
3-D 4-D 5-D (third, fourth and fifth dimensions)
All That Is, Ancient Aramaic, Ancient, Ancients, Ancestral Wisdom, Attention
Abundance, Being, Be, BE, Body-Mind-Heart, Breathe, Breathing
Conscious, Consciousness, Cosmos, Creator, Create
Evolutionary Leap, Leap, Freedom
Gamma, Great Master, Greater Mind
Heart, HUmanity -HUwomity
I Am, Journey, Life, Live, Living, Loving, Loved
Masters, New, Now
Observer-Creator, Oneness, Path, Planet
Quantum, Response-Ability
Smile, Smiling, Solar, Unity, Vibration
Vitality, Joy, Peace,
conscious-unconscious
dis-solve, dis-ease, dis-comfort, dis-integrate
in-formation, i-llnes
"reality," Response-Ability
space-time, time-space, timespace, spacetime
thought-emotion, we-llness, World

CONTENTS

PART 4 - BODY: Rejuvenation & Growing Younger with Healthy Eating, Cleanse & Detox

INTRODUCTION: *A Powerful Destiny*

Backed by science and chronicled by the Ancients, we are being irresistibly drawn into a surreal and empowering future, promising to carry us far beyond our wildest imaginings. We are Now riding the perfect wave into exciting new expressions of Health, Vitality, LOVE, Abundance and Co-Creation, as we merge with uncensored self-empowerment into a Newly Created *21st Century Superhuman* World.

> The possibility of stepping into a higher plane is quite real for everyone. It requires no force or effort or sacrifice. It involves little more than changing our ideas about what is normal.
>
> *Deepak Chopra MD*
> *Natural Physician, New Thought Author*

Grasp the magnitude of this: Celestial conjunctions that align only once every 26,000 years are activating our sense of Oneness with All Things. Earth's magnetics are lowest in 4,000 years, opening us to transformative shifts as *21st Century Superhumans*. Quantum physics, Now a frontrunner science, endorses the idea that magnetics, thought and emotion literally instantly reshape matter and events around us. The Heart is our most influential sending device (more powerful than the brain), and as we take a deep Breath, we realize the Ancients were right, the long prophesied *Shift of the Ages* is upon us...

What if this *Shift* predicted by the Ancients, rather than being a fearful cataclysm, guarantees answers to our most burning questions? What if New ways of thinking and Being turn painful health challenges, stressful economic struggles, fear, rage, sadness, corrupt banking, governments in turmoil, environment at risk into our *greatest triumph*?

This book is *the roadmap and breadcrumb trail* for this grand adventure! It *is the* Guidebook for our Now, to navigate looming personal and global crisis, launching us into the most thrilling Evolutionary Leap in human history, potentially as Life-changing as when humanity discovered language.

21st Century Superhuman is a potent manual, with step-by-step instructions, that effortlessly changes everything. It answers compelling questions about *who we are, why we're here and where we're going...* Join author Cary and associate Teddi, as they Light the way with smiles, twinkling eyes, and a flair for making the outrageous fun, with what could be the script for a wild sci-fi movie or fantasy adventure, yet this is *as "real" as it gets!*

> ...I didn't come here to tell you how this is going to end. I came here to tell you how it's going to begin... I'm going to show these people what you don't want them to see. I'm going to show them a world...without rules and controls, without borders or boundaries; a world where anything is possible.
>
> *Neo*
> *The Matrix*

Same content Now published in both original 500 page version and 4 Parts for ease of reading.

PREFACE: *Collective Awakening to Health, Abundance and LOVE*

This is *THE* Guidebook for a quickly approaching life-changing journey, as we teeter on the brink of an Evolutionary Leap called the *Shift of the Ages*. Within these pages are essential tools for powerful thought Creation, healthy living, vitality, abundance, LOVE and to shine in the World as our True *Essence*, for we are about to be transformed.

Breathe and Smile as you read, for there is much to absorb here, exposing a stunning New way of Being. There are four PARTS to the **21st Century Superhuman System:**

1. **SHIFT OF THE AGES: Cosmic Light & Ancient Texts meet Quantum Physics**

2. **MIND: The BEST Secret Formula to Manifest LOVE, Health, Abundance**

3. **SPIRIT: Live Your Dreams: Success, Passion, Relationship, Community**

4. **BODY: Rejuvenation & Growing Younger - Healthy Eating, Cleanse & Detox**

Each "PART" contains essential elements. Reading a little daily (whether you have the "big" book or four smaller ones) will provide deep integration of this essential material. Let your instincts lead. Your brain's capacity will increase, as expansive new insights become familiar. Mind-Heart-Body-Spirit adapt, as we put these concepts into practice in daily Life. As New brain cells and neurological pathways become activated, you may experience surges of vitality as well as the occasional need to rest more. Positive "rewiring" takes place, as we unravel old structures and beliefs. You will be amazed at what surprisingly fortunate doors miraculously open in your Life, when you collapse old belief systems.

This book is a "download" from "Greater Mind" by Cary Ellis, primary Author. She and Teddi Mulder have collaborated for many years. Teddi contributes her gift of telepathic "automatic writing - in italics and her energy graces the pages. Stretch your Mind, let go old constructs; then move, walk, play, Breathe, Smile and come back for more. Read anywhere and you'll be in the very right place. As you read we promise, you will not be the same person you were yesterday! Quantum principles, Now a Global groundswell are generating a massive wave! Join literally millions around the Planet utilizing these powerful Keys to up-level the entire human Journey. *Don't miss out joining in on the fun!!*

We are often asked, "Would someone *please* explain Quantum physics to me, so that I can understand it?" As Einstein said, "Unless you can explain it to a six year old, you don't understand it very well yourself." *This* is the launching pad, and it *is* a game-changer! *The Quantum journey requires opening the Mind to recognize that everything surrounding us emerges from thought. Wow!* This is a huge shift from thousands of years of thinking, "someone or something else is to blame." Pick up this book(s), read anywhere and you'll find the perfect input for " Now." Multiple readings activate more brain cells!

Transformation emerges from seeds planted; and soon you realize you are Jack or Jane climbing the Beanstalk into the clouds, looking back at the old Life far below, to which there will be no return, for the *treasure* lies ahead. We look forward to sharing this astounding journey with you, as we move together into brilliant expression far beyond what we've yet dreamed. As we escape the sleep-walk of millennia in this Collective Awakening, we discover greater expression of health, vitality, abundance and LOVE.

Physics isn't the most important thing - LOVE is.

Richard Feynman (1918-1988)
Nobel Prize Physics, Einstein Award

Welcome to what may appear more incredible than what you bargained for, yet once understood ultimately "the way." Join us to experience your Life transforming in mind-expanding and wonderful ways. Teetering on the brink of this ultimate Evolutionary Leap, we learn how to shed old self-destructive habits like water flying off a shaking dog.

Transformation of each Mind-Heart ignites this powerful change anew. Your participation is essential to the whole, so join with us on this adventure of a Lifetime, long called by prophets *Shift of the Ages*. Release old constructs; let them flow like molten lava into the archaeology of a distant past, freeing your spirit to soar in New ways!

Gather with others in this great collective Awakening, as with mutual inspiration you *"polish your shine."* As *we* build community spirit, *"where two or more are gathered"* miracles occur, and a rightly aligned Life reveals the clear path to Health, Abundance and LOVE.

We are grateful for extraordinary good fortune to share this amazing Journey; for as we step into expression of our True *Essence,* a new "reality" is born. We look forward to meeting you on the path, as shifting ourselves, we victoriously shift the entire Hologram!

LOVE and Blessings to All -

♥ *Cary & Teddi* ♥

Learning is finding out what you already know. Doing is demonstrating that you know it. Teaching is reminding others that they know just as well as you.
You are all learners, doers, and teachers.

Richard Bach
Illusions - Adventures of a Reluctant Messiah

FORWARD: *dr. michael ryce*

I have known Cary Ellis and Teddi Mulder for over 30 years, and have admired their commitment to growth and inquiry. I have encountered their minds researching and studying as I have myself over the years. Their approach offers essential keys to understanding, integrating and living a "whole" Life.

The adventure Cary and Teddi take us on is the path to elevating the entire being into wellness. Both Cary and her associate Teddi have lived and taught a true transformational healing journey for many years, and are about to share it with you. Prepare to enter an exceptional view from many levels of consciousness and well-being and be wowed! With 60 years plus of study between them, you will save yourself decades of reinventing the wheel. The years of research and wisdom each has tapped into in their lifework equals thousands.

On my path as a Naturopathic Physician I came to recognize that illness and aging were caused partially by our habits of everyday Life - yet even more so by the *root* of those habits in Mind and Heart. Whether our energy is freely flowing or inhibited by old unconscious thoughts and emotions of fear and hostility, plays a huge role in well-being.

> Thoughts give rise to neuropeptides and chemical reactions, which produce physiological results...in the mind-body connection every change in the mental-emotional state causes a change in body physiology and...energy manifesting into physical matter. Feelings are chemical. They can kill or cure.
>
> *Candace Pert PhD*
> *Brain Research Pioneer, "Molecules Of Emotion"*

Perhaps the ancients who said, "Perfect LOVE casts out fear" and "The first Law [of health and human existence] is LOVE," knew exactly what they were saying. Beyond thousands of generations of history built on believing "someone else is at fault," we are beginning to look within. Many generations of human civilization built on this false premise, set up a foundation for chronic misery now playing itself out in the World.

I have had privilege of close association with translation of one of the oldest Ancient Aramaic documents, that recorded Jesus' (or in his own language of Aramaic, Yeshua's) actual teachings. Rather than a religious language, Aramaic is language of quantum physics. What Yeshua came to share with us is the most healing message on the planet today when rightly understood. *True Forgiveness* is not about letting someone else "off the hook" or pardoning. It is about removing anything within ourselves Not of LOVE that is resonating into form our current "reality." Once understood, shifting at this level is the wellspring of a Life of vitality, energy, creativity, joy and well-being.

> What controls the composition of your blood, and therefore the fate of your cells? ...signals from the environment...interpreted by the mind... The brain releases chemistry into the blood that controls cell behavior and genetic activity. If you change your belief and perception, you can change the chemistry of your blood and Create your own biology.
>
> *Bruce Lipton, PhD*
> *Biology of Belief*

I have the highest respect for Cary and Teddi, whose lives are dedicated to living and teaching principles of practical everyday guidelines to awakening from the inside, while bringing Lifestyle practices into harmony with a path of Lightness and Well-Being.

This handbook is an amazing reference and guide for the home, family or individual seeking to refine Lifestyle with progressive mental and physical habits and tools. It addresses how we foundationally shift to the kind of true Life that flows from clear Mind, Heart and Soul, taking self-responsibility for our Creations to restore our True Design LOVE. The effort taken to adopt this New "enlightened" way of living will be well worth it, bearing fruit in greater Life and Vitality.

> The moment you change your perception is the moment
> you re-write the chemistry of your body.
>
> *Bruce Lipton, PhD*

And then, who knows what you will do with so much energy? Perhaps live the Life of your dreams... May you be blessed in your journey. We hold the space for every Mind, Heart and Being on the planet to live in radiance and well-being, flowing from returning to our *Essence - Pure LOVE.*

LOVE to You - You are LOVED.

♥ dr. michael ryce ♥

"Why Is This Happening to Me... Again?!"
Landmark work with Khaburis Manuscript
Ancient Aramaic Forgiveness
WhyAgain dot org

ACKNOWLEDGMENT

Here we stand on the shoulders of giants...
by Cary Ellis DD with Theodora Mulder PhD

21st Century Superhuman, Quantum Lifestyle is a product of many productive years in the *Field*. Our wonderful teachers to whom credit is due, exposed us to vital truth founded in natural order and Universal Law. Much Gratitude goes out to those who guided us with their Presence through books, teachings and practical application. Many of these evolutionary Wisdom Keepers have now transitioned from this Life, after imparting timeless knowledge to us, to be passed on to you and *so the circle continues.*

We are honored to have been initiated into respected lineages that carried powerful truth forward. Notice when *you* are being blessed to participate in a Truth-carrying Lineage. Tony Robbins says, *"We Model Excellence by sitting at the feet of Masters;* duplicating their physiology and mental syntax we access the same part of our brain that they do."

The *Essence* of those who gifted us with their guidance continues today, with practical tools, systems and resources, transforming us and our World...

THOSE WHO HAVE GONE ON TO BE WITH US IN SPIRIT

Dr. Ann Wigmore, Founder, Hippocrates wheatgrass and living foods programs, honorary "grandmother" of today's raw food movement

Rev. Don Haughey, Founder, Creative Health Institute (formerly Hippocrates)

Dr. John Whitman Ray Founder Body Electronics: Health and the Human Mind, Body/ Spinal/Cranial Electronics and associated Iridology

Dr. Max Gerson, Founder, Gerson Cancer Therapy, his daughter **Charlotte Gerson** (still living) and the ongoing work of Gerson Cancer Therapy Inst.

Bernard Jensen, DC, Iridology pioneer, body cleansing and detoxification

Dr. Christopher Hills, Founder Light Force Spirulina as a primary food source, enough food for all; University of the Trees; President, World Yoga Society

Dr. Hanna Kroeger, Master Herbalist

Sun Bear, Native American Shaman, Wisdom Teachings and Visionary

Jack White, Spiritual Educator, author *God's Game of Life*

Nellie and Ed Cain, Teachings on Universal Laws of the Kabbalah, author *Exploring the Mysteries of Life*

Drs. Marion and Mikele McCumber, Bishop of the Church of Tzaddi

Dr. Thomas Stone, Psychiatry, Environmental Medicine, pioneer in resolving brain disorders caused by environmental sensitivity and food allergies

Daniel Dieska, D.D.S. Holistic Dentistry

D.A. Versendaal, D.C., Educator, Innovator Applied Kinesiology, Contact Reflex Analysis CRA and Applied Trophology

James V. Goure Founder, United Research, Inc. & The Light Center. *"Mission:* To increase awareness of Oneness of All That Is by expanding Light, Peace & unconditional Love." Atomic Energy Commission 1947-75 which lead to healing the Planet w/prayers for Peace.

THOSE HERE DOING THEIR WONDERFUL WORK

Gregg Braden Author - *Divine Matrix, Awakening to Zero Point, Walking Between the Worlds,* and many more

Dr. Bruce Lipton *The Biology of Belief; Spontaneous Evolution* w/ Steve Bhaerman

dr. michael ryce Ancient Aramaic Forgiveness, *Why is this Happening to me Again?*

Dr. Richard Bartlett & Melissa Joy Matrix Energetics

Viktoras Kulvinskas *Survival into the 21st Century,* Co-Founder Hippocrates Health Inst.

Amrit Desai - Founder Kripalu Yoga

Anthony Robbins, Firewalking, Personal Power, NLP

John Davis, Coptics International TheCopticCenter dot org & SpiritualUnityofNations dot org, World Service Order

Dolphins, Whales, Animals, Earth Mother Gaia - ALL in our miraculous natural World

Additionally - Essene Gospels; Ram Dass; Parmahansa Yogananda; Garret John LoPorto; Roy Eugene Davis; Margaret Mead; Barbara Marx Hubbard; Jean Houston; Kryon; John Lennon; Drunvalo Melchizedek; Dieter Broers; David Wilcock; David Icke; Stephen Hawking; Barbara Marciniak; Ken Carey; Zecharia Sitchin; Peace Pilgrim; HeartMath Institute; Nassim Haramein; Michael Tellinger; Graham Hancock; Sacha Stone; Eckhart Tolle; John, Deo and Ocean Robbins; David Spangler; Peter and Eileen Caddy; Dean and Mary Hardy; Carl and Ortrun Franklin; Machalle Wright; Byron Katie; *Abraham Teachings* with Jerry and Esther Hicks; the family of HUmanity-HUwomity; Ascended Masters, Angels of Light, Great White & Rainbow Brotherhood, Beings of LIGHT and LOVE *in all dimensions.* We thank our families, LOVED ones, pets, friends and ancestors present and in Spirit from whose lives, passages and continuing presence we learn so much.

We are grateful to all gifted ones quoted here. Each showed up in an amazing way, as if to say, "I gave my life for freedom, enlightenment and empowerment of humanity, add me," as their perfect quote immediately appeared!

We grow daily as part of a Heart-centered *"Global Mastermind,"* Now transmitted with lightening-speed around the Planet. It is no longer possible to keep track of what ignites our inspiration. Excited to be part of this unfolding, millions are Now shifting Worldwide into an awakened state. The astounding News that that *only* way to change things on the outside is to shift ourselves on the inside to LOVE, is Now spreading like wildfire!!!

We are blessed, inspired and uplifted, to be moving into True Unity among humankind. Carl Johan Calleman, who left a prestigious scientific career to research the Mayan Calendar full time, offers its premise for our times:

> May we inspire You to feel like You
> are an integral part of the Universe.

~ 21st CENTURY SUPERHUMAN ~

Breathe - Smile

Rest - Movement

Cleanse and Detox

Moderation in All Things

Purify with Water Inside and Out

Meditate - Merge with the *Field*

Nourish with High Frequency Foods

Align with Your True Design, LOVE

Mind & Emotion Marry in the Heart

There Is No 'Out There' Out There

Our Thoughts Create Our "Reality"

Compassion without Judgment

Clean Out the Unconscious

Cancel, Release, Let Go

Gratitude - Thank You

Mud Between the Toes

KNOW it IS [Done]

Be Your Prayers

Live Your Truth

Heart Coherence

Enjoy the Journey

Honor Others' Choices

Laugh, Smile, Dance and Play

Live Your Essence

Leap for Joy

BE at Peace

♥ LOVE ♥

www.21stCenturySuperhuman.com

The joy is that we can take back our bodies,
reclaim our health,
and restore ourselves to balance.
We can take power over what and how we eat.
We can rejuvenate and recharge ourselves,
bringing healing
to the wounds we carry inside us,
and bringing to fuller life
the wonderful person
that each of us can be.

John Robbins
FoodRevolution dot org

Part 4 Body: Section 1
Back To The Garden

You may say I'm a dreamer, but I'm not the only one.
I hope someday you'll join us. And the world will live as one.

John Lennon
Imagine

Viktoras Kulvinskas published *Survival Into The 21st Century: Planetary Healers Manual* in 1972, and it came to us as a shining Light, guiding our way into greater awakening. Forerunner for our times, it held in-spiration and in-formation that helped us shape our lives. It pointed the way to learn and expand our horizons, resulting in many adventures in well-being and consciousness. I (Cary) had the great opportunity to spend time with Viktoras, living and learning on his Connecticut farm, which was wonderful and enlightening.

Seeking his own wellness Viktoras had discovered the natural path of fasting and raw foods, and in 1968 co-founded the Boston Hippocrates Institute with Dr. Ann Wigmore (1909-1993). His story of personal regeneration was ultimately inspiring. A pure mathematician and highly respected computer programmer, his book came forth as a brilliant detailed "data-dump" of his cosmic awakenings *and* recognition of what a truly healthy Life-path is. On the cover was hot pink Peter Max visionary art, with hand-done drawings throughout the book. Though the style was unconventional, it went out like wildfire *(still available online)*, as valuable a reference guide today as it was then. We *highly* recommend owning it, as it contains valuable details on thriving and surviving in our World, healthy concepts, wisdom-based tools, resources and foundational teachings around living foods, cleansing, regeneration and community.

Very rarely in Life does one encounter a book with the magnitude of Viktoras Kulvinskas' *Survival in the 21st Century*. Within it's pages, LOVE consciousness springs forth from a master of body ecology. Viktoras' pioneering work has touched so many people, it is considered by many as a "new age bible" in the holistic and health field. Few can resist the wisdom and experience this buried treasure shares and although Survival was written 27 years ago, one would be amazed at how time stands still within it's pages.

Darksunblade, Review at amazon.com

We initiate this part of our book with Viktoras, because *Survival into the 21st Century* was such a powerful springboard for us, landing us right where we are today. It is about vital connection with Earth, Sky and Heart. It inspires us to tap into *Essence* within ourselves, cultivating intelligent Survival, and beyond that our Thriving.

This place you are right now God circled on a map for you.

Hafiz, 14th Century Persian Mystic Poet

I NOW AFFIRM: I Am restoring my True Design LOVE and *Essence.* As I clear my Mind-Heart to Live this path, friends, family, community and relationships harmonize around my "reality." Synchronicities occur and doors open for the good of all.

You can survive. The spirit is timeless... I present ways to survive and prepare for the New World to come. Be not dismayed when you seem to be alone in the pursuit. Remember, "Few are chosen." Your close friends and members of your family may ridicule you. Let them not offend or provoke you. LOVE them just the same - do not fight back. Teach others by your example, not with empty words. "You shall know them by their deeds."

Viktoras Kulvinskas
Survival Into The 21st Century - Planetary Healers Manual (1975)

In 1969 at Yasgur's farm in upstate New York 32 bands and 400,000, "initiated" an "age" at *Woodstock,* opening Minds to a radical New way of Life. Crosby, Stills, Nash and Young prophetically sang, "We are caught in the devil's bargain," with unspoken hunger for that which seemed lost...

Well, then can I walk beside you? I have come here to lose the smog.
I feel like I am a cog in something turning.
And maybe it's the time of year, yes, maybe it's the time of man.
Got to get back to the land and set my Soul free
We are stardust, we are golden, we are billion year old carbon,
And we got to get ourselves back to the garden.

How we step into and express our Lives is critical to the Whole, for as Rumi says, *"Be relentless in your looking, because you are the one you seek."* In our deepest longings we discover vital keys to authentically reclaiming *SELF.* Taking clues we've been given, *21st Century Superhumans* enter a New way of Living, heightening self-expression and Well-Being. Ultimately we'll say, *"Thank you"* for this **Quantum Lifestyle** path laid out before us. You Now reading have begun to activate self-knowledge leading the way to En-Light-enment. Proper, natural care of the Body is foundational to this laudable Journey. ♥

18

Part 4: BODY

Chapter 1

Choosing Your Approach to Wellness

All you need is LOVE. But a little
chocolate now and then doesn't hurt.

Charles M. Schulz (1992-2000)
Creator of" Peanuts"

How Body is nourished is one of the most nurturing and delicious topics to take place anywhere on Earth any day, despite the fact *some* know we *can* Live on *Prana* or Light. It is said we can get along for a week without laughter, yet if we were without food for that long most would grumble, though a short fast generally does us good. We may go days without laughter yet it is wonderfully beneficial. Robert T. Meuller PhD tells us, "The average

kindergartener laughs 300x/day, average adult 17." Let's laugh more! Choosing a healthy Lifestyle *through-time* is better than suddenly adopting it when things "go wrong."

We are moving beyond the belief that the only way the physical changes, is by changing the physical, which has been our working 3-D model. This is a "world is flat" philosophy. Bruce Lipton reminds us that Newtonian Physics says the World is made out of mechanical parts: the basis of medicine-when broken change the parts with chemicals, surgery and drugs. Quantum physics says everything is a *Field* in which we are immersed and the Field controls Biology. *The Field is the sole governing agency of the particle.* (Einstein)

Quantum Reality: If everything we do and think is the byproduct of how we perceive the information (our reality bias) then it implies, that by adequately reordering our perceptions, we affect the outcome of everything in our lives.

Dr. Richard Bartlett
Matrix Energetics.

Studies Now show we can change the Body with thought. In his book, *Healing Back Pain: The Mind Body Connection,* back surgeon Dr. John Sarno tells us that *most back problems can be solved by clearing associated thought-emotional issues;* in 95% of cases, surgery is not required. The theory "if we 'eat right' we'll be healthy" is Newtonian. Physical is subject to thought resonating through the *Field*. Quantum physics tells us Life and Well-being emerge from Perception, Attitude and Belief. When these change, everything changes.

Powerful documentary *Water: The Great Mystery* by Les Sundeen, documents that water permeating our World has memory and carries thought. Shifting into LOVE, our thought-energy transmitted through water in the air and our Bodies, transforms us and our World. (Body 75-80% water, Earth's surface 70%). In 1472 a dedicated Abbott was imprisoned and given a crust of stale bread and dipper of stinking water daily. After 40 days he had gained health and strength. Extorted from him under *torture* he confessed he had "prayed over the water, giving thanks for what he had," and as he did so the water turned sweet and clear.

Thought links us to the fabric of Creation. We are the "pharmacist," instructing our endocrine system what chemicals to produce. As we operate in LOVE and Heart Coherence we change our internal chemistry, we awaken DNA, increase Longevity and Well-Being. Tibetan monks repeat prayers till water in the Body harmonizes to clear ailments. Prayers measure 7.8-8.6 Hz. matching Earth's resonance.

When dealing with illness in self or family members, adopting a healthy Quantum Lifestyle helps build a new foundation. Additionally benefits of modern medicine may assist to remedy a critical state, to give the Body a jump on recovery. Ultimately the wise human civilization will combine medical advancements with the amazing bounty of natural practices and remedies available, which we cover in this book. Such choices are personal and should be made with both research and listening to the Body and intuition. Leading example of combining holistic with the medical approach is the *Mercy Health Wege Institute for Mind, Body and Spirit* in Grand Rapids, Michigan, with the Mission:

> ...offering effective, individualized, patient care for mind, body and spirit, we both complete and enhance mainstream medical care by partnering progressive complementary therapies with mainstream medical services and practitioners.
>
> This integrative approach is a valuable resource for those who wish to increase self-awareness, enhance overall well being and prevent future health issues, as well as those who are chronically ill.

Coming chapters take us into Natural Body care. It *does* matter what we eat and how we nourish ourselves. It also matters what kind of Mind-energy we hold around water, food and Life, for in so doing we are literally creating the substance of our Body and our World, our state of well-being and our relationship with the Web of Life. ♥

> Your Life does matter. It always matters whether you reach out in friendship or lash out in anger. It always matters whether you live with compassion and awareness or whether you succumb to distractions and trivia. It always matters how you treat other people, how you treat animals, and how you treat yourself. It always matters what you do. It always matters what you say. And it always matters what you eat.
>
> John Robbins
> *The Food Revolution: How Your Diet Can Help Save Your Life and Our World*

Part 4: BODY

Chapter 2

How Thought Affects The Body

Your health is what you make of it. Everything you do and think either adds to the vitality, energy and spirit you possess, or takes away from it.

Dr. Ann Wigmore (1909-1993)
"Grandmother" of Wheatgrass - Living Foods

Tibetan Monks of the Dalai Lama's lineage followed detailed Ancient Traditions over thousands of years, perfecting mantras to influence weather and World conditions. They report that "When we have a pure heart and sound our mantras correctly, the 'Lord of the water' brings us rain." They are living repositories of very specific Ancient knowledge of the science of how we operate in this World. Accessing Heart Coherence through deep Compassion without judgment, their sacred, effective mantra-prayer is based in Quantum physics!

Another example of Ancient knowledge offers affects of prayer on the physical. In 1991 in a desperate two year drought, Israel's only freshwater lake was critically low. So 10,000 Israelis gathered at the Wailing Wall, *chanted and prayed rain;* within 3 days rain came in torrents. A rabbi explained their religion's traditions are designed *to affect the outcome;* and those who call this "coincidence" are not interested in Living True Response-Ability.

> Not a single scientist who is familiar with systems theory doubts [shifting the physical with prayer]. It is entirely a question of waiting for a moment when the system is in a state of instability. In a phase of instability, the motion of thought alone is sufficient for the system to start to change.
>
> Gerbert Klima, Professor of Inst. Nuclear Physics, Vienna Austria
> Water: The Great Mystery by Les Sundeen

We've experienced affirming the sky is clear and blue on a day when "chemtrails" were filling the sky, and within minutes the sky was perfectly clear. Alternate reality?

HeartMath® research reveals that a person in *Heart Coherence* literally turns on codons in their own and others DNA, offering powerful insight into the Evolutionary Leap in which we are Now engaged. HeartMath® finds measurable Heart Coherence is Created by Deep LOVE, Compassion and Gratitude. Literally in simple terms, *all* that is needed to shift health, well-being, and our World, is clearing Not of LOVE thought-emotional patterns, to our True Design LOVE (covered in detail Part 2: MIND). Clearing Now. Breathe. Smile.

> Beautify your thoughts. Thoughts are the headwaters
> of action, life and manifestation.
>
> David Wolfe
> *The Sunfood Diet Success System*

It's amazing we Now have the understanding of exactly how these powerful keys work to transform us as **21st Century Superhumans** and our World! It's not rocket science, yet it is a complete turnaround from how we've been thinking and Living the last many thousand years! The instant we change, *everything* changes. This is Universal Law number two – Law of Correspondence, *"As above, so below, as below, so above"* - the same pattern expresses on all planes of existence from the smallest electron to the largest star and vice versa. Shift ourselves - shift the entire Hologram. *Arc the Hologram Now with LOVE.*

> We live at the threshold of Universal recognition
> that the human being is not mere matter,
> but a potent, energetic, field of consciousness.
>
> *Michael Beckwith, New Thought Minister*
> *Founder Agape International Spiritual Center, 8,000 members*

Energy pattern found throughout Creation called a torus field, recorded in Ancient petroglyphs and described in Sacred Geometry promises to be our source of infinitely abundant, clean, free energy based on today's cutting edge innovations. The doughnut shaped torus field spins and implodes in on itself continuously, creating a gravity vortex. Quantum physicist Nassim Haramein hints that within the gravity of black holes we actually may discover LOVE or Source, holding Creation in form.

Our HEART is located in the central vortex of our own torus field. As we resonate LOVE, Compassion and Gratitude into the World through the Heart, our spinning torus field expands, sending our resonance powerfully into our cells and the surrounding field. It shrinks when relating with Not of LOVE thoughts or emotions, and it can extend out to 8-12' to *miles* when we resonate Deep LOVE, Compassion and Gratitude. As we tune our Heart with coherent emotions, we, our bodies and our World emerge into New regenerative form.

Dr. Berrenda Fox, naturopath and holistic practitioner at Avalon Wellness Centre in Mt. Shasta, California and advisor for television shows about UFO contact, works with children born with additionally activated DNA strands, which she says is becoming quite common. "These children can move objects across the room just by concentrating on them and can fill a glass of water just by looking at it." This type of DNA change is also happening in adults Now moving into in LOVE.

These extraordinary children show New potential with more DNA activated. They tend to be able to instantly correct issues that may have previously seemed "unsolvable." They naturally shift self and World in extraordinary ways, easily solving *seemingly* overwhelming "problems" with Mind and Heart. These children bear witness to higher potentials, already within *us* for self-healing, regeneration and radiant Living. Be sure to learn how to fully activate these levels in yourself, throughout all 4 Parts of this *21st Century Superhuman* series, videos and more at our website.

Dr. Fox tells us we are transitioning from a carbon based body structure that we've had for thousands of years, to a crystalline structure, to easily navigate and adapt to Higher dimensions. Some are beginning to exhibit this New Light Body. Remember, Not of LOVE Mind-energy is like a "logjam," that solidifies or crystalizes in the body, slowing down Life-force. Dissolving this density, first we shed water-tears, then vapor. As we increase our capacity to resonate LOVE, Gratitude, Compassion in ALL situations, ALL that is Not of LOVE vaporizes, and we and our entire World move into frequencies of higher dimensional existence. Heeding our language is highly critical in to our DNA. Words carry vibrational resonance, shaping us and our "reality." *Speak every word as Conscious Creator.* Vibrational resonance of every word matters.

..how many DNA strands are we capable of possessing? Some geneticists are claiming humans will one day have 12 strands.

Dr. Fox says, "There are major changes and mutations occurring in our DNA. We are evolving. "We will be developing twelve helixes. During this time, which seems to have started 5 to 20 years ago, we have been mutating...into something for which the end result is not yet known."

...DNA holds genetic codes for physical and emotional evolution through frequency held in languages we speak....Russian linguists found that the genetic code, especially in the apparently useless junk DNA, follows the same rules as all our human language...our DNA follows a regular grammar...like our languages. So human languages did not appear coincidentally but are a reflection of our inherent DNA [and vice versa].

Russian biophysicist and molecular biologist Pjotr Garjajev...explored Vibrational behavior of DNA. "Living chromosomes function just like solitonic/ holographic computers..." This explains why affirmations, autogenous training [such as our upcoming goal canceling] and hypnosis have such strong effects on humans and our bodies. *It is entirely normal and natural for our DNA to react to language....*

During this time in the 75,000 year cycle, we are now exposed to the most torsion energy waves, affecting our DNA, reorganizing the 97% "junk" DNA from 2-strand double helix to a 12-strand helix, advancing humanity in a leap of evolution.

Marco Torres
Scientists Finally Present Evidence On Expanding DNA Strands

Heart Coherence, based in the state of Deep LOVE, Compassion , Gratitude is one of the single most effective keys for *21st Century Superhumans* to implement! [Discussed at length in Part 2: MIND]. As we clear the unconscious, activating this state, we establish new neurological pathways transforming our entire Vibrational context to LOVE. HeartMath® offers an app with sensory-feedback unit for iPhone and computer. Users report use for 15-20 minutes a day for 2-3 weeks achieves Heart Coherence. This is an easy tool to use, share with friends, family or organization, to transform Life with simple Heart Coherence.

Our Heart's torus field sends out a more expansive resonance when Coherent in LOVE, Compassion, Gratitude. Heart Coherence hugely shifts personal issues and energies, as a result shifts the entire collective. Focusing Mind-Energy in LOVE, turns on DNA codons and empowers our visions and dreams. Accessing Heart Coherence "changes our World," *Arc the Hologram with LOVE!*

We do not experience things as they really are! We experience them only through a filter, which determines what information will enter our awareness and what will be rejected. If we change the filter [our content or belief system], we automatically experience the world in a completely different way.

David Wolfe
The Sunfood Diet Success System

When *fear* and *hostility* bathe our cells with their chemicals, unless we shift this resonance, acidity, inflammation and circulating sticky material called fibrins eventually cause toxemia that results in dis-ease and death. It is essential to clear our thought-emotional patterns in order to restore Heart Coherence. Our Emotional Tone Scale in Part 3: SPIRIT, is of great assistance to keep us moving upscale toward Joy and Enthusiasm.

Even our WORDS Create a Living resonance in our World. The Original Language, called the Language of Light, contained literally vibrational patterns that called Creation into Being. Ancient Languages such as Aramaic, Sanskrit, Hebrew, Lakota and others contain much of this original resonance, some of which has been lost in our modern languaging. However, nevertheless, Every Word We Speak sends its resonance into the World whether to Create or destroy. Language has also been made confusing with too many meaningless words such as "the" to remove us from flowing with Creation.

BEING AWARE OF EVERY WORD is a powerful **21st Century Superhuman** trait. We KNOW Every Word carries creative thought resonance, holding Attention on the *Field*. Choosing our Words well is a *VITAL PRACTICE*, supporting clearing of old data [Part 2: MIND] to change our "reality" Now. Besides the obvious hurtful words, weed out those such as but, might, must, can, could would, wish, time and hope. Cultivate thought and Words along the lines of "I Am," aligned with continual flow of Creation from the *Field*.

Powerful resources are readily available to re-tool our thought pathways. If you have not already done this vital personal realignment of your Words, grab some books or audios and zip through them to ground your Vital Positively Productive Mind-Heart-Voice. Our all time favorites include Godfrey Ray King's *I Am Discourses* from the 1930s. Louise Hay's *You Can Heal Your Life* and many more, with thoughts and affirmations for Positive Creation. The *Abraham* work of Jerry and Esther Hicks has also opened up profound ideas.

Learn to clarify how to use your Words, to assist with clearing old data from the unconscious, to present the powerful energy of your Mind-Heart to the *Field* to Create in New ways! Proper use of Words supports removing our old data or content Not of LOVE from the unconscious, using our *Ancient Aramaic* clearing techniques. Another excellent supportive tool is EFT-tapping, which helps ground in our neurobiology this work we are doing. Be sure to read Part 2: MIND to fully grasp what we are discussing here.

Now, Ideal Nutrition and physical Cleanse and Detox, along with clearing Mind-Heart, totally shifts our internal chemistry with renewed focus on LOVE. This complete-person "waking up" is a Journey of the **21st Century Superhuman.** As we enter this clearing it's common to have all-encompassing waves of Not of LOVE offload from thousands of generations. Dredging up old layers stored in "carbon-based-memory" of the unconscious, we are Now installing a new "operating system" founded in our True Design LOVE.

Now, Rather than going in to old reactive patterns or suppressing what's uncomfortable, our New way of Being in the World, notices what comes up, clears it on the spot, and we go right back into our natural state of Pure LOVE, Breathing and Smiling. Those on the cutting edge of "food and consciousness," know that True High Frequency Living incorporates Food and Cleansing, and equally essential Mind-Heart. "Rock star of the superfood World," David Wolfe says:

> The world we think we see is only a view, a collective description of the world that we Create through our belief systems. Accepting this fact seems to be one of the most empowering things one can do.
>
> David Wolfe
> *Sunfood Diet Success System*

Always vigilant, we recognize the dominant role thought-emotion plays a in what Creates our state of Being. Tony Robbins taught us *everything is about "State."* It determines what kind of fluids our body's cells are bathed in, how we make food and life choices, and whether our Life is in a chronic state of covering up what bothers us, or opening to Greater LOVE, *Essence* and Well-Being. Our state of Mind-Heart is a key determinant to well-being.

> It's not correct to see yourself as an isolated organism in time and space, occupying 6 ft.³ of volume, lasting seven or eight decades. Rather, you are one cell in the cosmic body entitled to all privileges of cosmic status including perfect health. Nature made us thinkers so we could realize this truth.
>
> *Deepak Chopra MD*
> *Perfect Health*

In the beginning we approach "getting what we desire" from the "outside:" "I'd like to heal ___, or I'd like to look better___, there's an area I'd like to improve, have a better relationship, more money, be more healthy." We plead, affirm, cajole, command, wish, hope with our 5% conscious thought (Harvard studies). The amazing thing is, once we go *deeper "inside,"* we discover that the entire World around us emanates from *within*, based on state of Mind-Heart (conscious-unconscious). Once we use our tools to go *inside* Mind-Heart, to view and alter things from *this* vantage point, we discover and align with how our resonance shapes what comes into Being around us. *[Covered extensively in Part 2: MIND]*

Much as we desire to send "healthy, productive" messages to our body, we still must clear our 95% unconscious thought so messages get to our body in the form we truly desire. Becoming Beings of LOVE, Compassion and Gratitude with every Breath, every Word, every Thought, every Action...ups the ante for ultimate well-being. So where is the *power* when we would like to "lose" weight, or "heal" from a dis-ease? Is it in the *food?* Is it in *how and when we eat? Healing methods?* It all *begins* with Mind-Heart Energy (conscious-unconscious), and how these qualify Creation of our "reality," as even physical choices emerge from it.

At the current vibrational state of our Body, water is a key thought transmitter that permeates our World. Centered in LOVE, more Light shows up in reflecting off of moisture surrounding us (as in image above). As we "cleanse and feed our our Living house" and settle into knowing ourselves as Divine Creator Beings of LOVE, Compassion and Gratitude Living in Truth and Authenticity, ALL in our World and our Body transforms. Thus the **21st Century Superhuman**, with Power of Coherent thought, activates our Evolving DNA in this Evolutionary Leap called *Shift of the Ages.* [Part 1] ♥

Part 4: BODY

Chapter 3

What Is Ideal Nutrition?

*Every aspect of our lives is, in a sense,
a vote for the kind of world we want to live in.*

Frances Moore Lappé
Diet for A Small Planet

Vegan, Vegetarian, Lacto-Vegetarian, Ovo-Vegetarian, Lacto-Ovo-Vegetarian, Omnivore, Paleo, Carnivore, Pescetarian, Flexitarian, Eat for Your Blood Type, Macrobiotic, Fruitarian, Breatharian, confused? Rather than saying exactly what the *right* diet *is*, let's review cutting edge data for you to make your own educated choices. It's easy to be attached to familiar habits, caught between old conditioning and New ideas so let's consider current research. Choices they can be gradual, unless recovery from illness is at hand.

The 4th Universal Law of Polarity, states that two opposites are different Vibrational frequencies of the same energy, "all truths are but half-truths, all paradoxes may be reconciled." A Master changes the form of opposites, by changing Mind-Energy to achieve balance. We've observed that exploring the opposite is a way of discovering balance, which often is part of the learning curve. *[Universal Laws Part 1: SHIFT OF THE AGES]*

An alchemist is one who transforms everything with LOVE.

Emmanuel Dagher
Co-Creating Miracles

Based on the Law of Cause and Effect, we might call habits enhancing vitality within the body systems a *live-it*, and habits that reduce flow of energy within body systems a *die-it*. Even so, the live-it or die-it we choose, is going to be a product of our Mind-energy.

It is no secret that most chronic dis-eases result from high-fat, sugar and over-processed foods of the standard American diet or SAD, consumed in most developed nations. A glance at statistics causes us to wonder why anyone would continue following this diet, however based on advertising of food production industry and pharmaceutical companies, many are obviously convinced that it's okay to over-consume, then medicate, that one can circumvent nature and get "fixed" when something goes amiss.

The food you eat can be either the safest and most powerful form of medicine or the slowest form of poison.

Ann Wigmore
Founder Original Hippocrates Health Institute-Wheatgrass and Living Foods

The Center for Dis-Ease Control reported out of 2.5 million deaths in the U.S. in 2010 almost half were caused by heart dis-ease and cancer. Heart dis-ease is the leading cause, though both are very close. *Here are statistics per year:*
  • Heart dis-ease: 597,689
  • Cancer: 574,743
  • Chronic lower respiratory dis-eases: 138,080
  • Stroke (cerebrovascular dis-eases): 129,476
  • Accidents (unintentional injuries): 120,859
  • Alzheimer's dis-ease: 83,494
  • Diabetes: 69,071
  • Nephritis, nephrotic syndrome, and nephrosis: 50,476
  • Influenza and Pneumonia: 50,097

 The World Health Organization reported in 2011 that *two thirds* of 55 million deaths Globally were due to non-communicable dis-eases, cardiovascular, cancer, diabetes and chronic lung dis-ease; with 87% of deaths in high income countries attributed to cardiovascular issues, including stroke and heart attack.

The beef industry has contributed to more American deaths than all the wars of this century, all natural disasters, and all automobile accidents combined.

Dr. Neal Barnard
Go Healthy Go Vegan Cookbook

USDA reports 62% of Americans are overweight, 27% classified as obese (30 pounds overweight), with an alarming trend toward obesity in children. Convenience foods increased cheese consumption from 7.7 pounds per person per year in the 1950s to 29.8 pounds in 2000; meat consumption 195 pounds in 2,000, up from 57 pounds per year during the 1950s. Might we call this "slow suicide"?

If beef is your idea of 'real food for real people,'
you'd better live real close to a real good hospital.

Dr. Neal Barnard
Prevent and Reverse Heart Disease

Fast Food Statistics website reports 160,000 fast food restaurants in America with 50 million served daily (2012). Annual North American fast food revenue, $110 *Billion.* Fast food contains more fat, calories, sugar, sodium, and less nutrition and vitamins.

> Chicken fat, beef fat, fish fat, fried foods - these are the foods that fuel our fat genes by giving them raw materials for building body fat.
>
> *Dr. Neal Barnard*
> *Author of Turn Off the Fat Genes*

With a glance at statistics above and what follows, we might wonder why we don't run the other way as fast as we can? What suppressive Mind-Energy perpetuates this cycle? Let's familiarize ourselves with landmark research of the last quarter-century, on prevention and reversal of degenerative conditions as a product of dietary choices. In Part 2: MIND we covered in detail how thoughts play an intrinsic role in wellness and illness.

> I believe that coronary artery dis-ease is preventable and that even after it is underway, its progress can be stopped, its insidious effects reversed. I believe, and my work over the past twenty years has demonstrated that all this can be accomplished without expensive mechanical intervention and with minimal use of drugs. The key lies in nutrition - specifically, in abandoning the toxic American diet and maintaining cholesterol levels well below those historically recommended by health policy experts.
>
> *Dr. Caldwell Esselstyn*
> *Prevent and Reverse Heart Disease*

Internationally known surgeon, researcher, and former clinician at the Cleveland Clinic, Dr. Caldwell Esselstyn put patients who had less than a year to live on a plant-based, fat-free diet. He prevented and reversed progression of heart dis-ease. Patients who stuck with the program improved dramatically, twenty years later remaining symptom-free. For those ready to to change Lifestyle habits, it's documented in his NY Times bestseller, *Prevent and Reverse Heart Disease,* with recipes for heart-healthy plant-based diet.

> Every mouthful of oils and animal products, including dairy foods, initiates an assault on these [cell] membranes and, therefore, on the cells they protect. These foods produce a cascade of free radicals in our bodies - especially harmful chemical substances that induce metabolic injuries from which there is only a partial recovery. Year after year, the effects accumulate. And eventually, the cumulative cell injury is great enough to become obvious, to express itself as what physicians define as dis-ease.
>
> Plants and grains do not induce the deadly cascade of free radicals. In fact, they carry an antidote. Unlike oils and animal products, they contain antioxidants, which help to neutralize the free radicals and also, recent research suggests, may provide considerable protection against cancer.
>
> *Dr. Caldwell Esselstyn*
> *Prevent and Reverse Heart Disease*

Dr. Esselstyn is a featured expert in the acclaimed documentary *Forks Over Knives*. His work has helped thousands, with his book behind Bill Clinton's Life-changing vegan diet. His book *Prevent and Reverse Heart Dis-Ease* explains the science behind the simple plan that changed the lives of his heart dis-ease patients forever, empowering readers with tools to take control of their Heart health.

> And it's not just a matter of bad information. The truth is that we are addicted to fat - literally. Receptors in our brains account for our addiction to nicotine, heroin, and cocaine, and similar cravings have been identified for fat and sugars as well.
>
> *Dr. Caldwell Esselstyn*
> *Prevent and Reverse Heart Disease*

Reading Dr. Caldwell's book encouraged *us* to take a look at consumption of healthy free fats and oils (refined-extracted not a whole food), minimizing olive and coconut oils, instead to good benefit, relying on *whole raw* nuts, seeds, avocado. For vegans and vegetarians whole food with a little healthy fat is okay. Soaking nuts and seeds starts sprouting and brings them to Life. Westin Price discovered healing elements in certain fats such as butter and cod liver oil, as he traveled the World searching for secrets to good health. He found nothing replaces natural unprocessed foods (Price-Pottenger Foundation).

> ...[oils] are not heart healthy. Between 14 and 17 percent of olive oil is saturated, artery-clogging fat - every bit as aggressive in promoting heart dis-ease as the saturated fat in roast beef. And even though a Mediterranean-style diet that allows such oils may slow the rate of progression of coronary heart dis-ease, when compared with diets even higher in saturated fat, it does not arrest the dis-ease and reverse its effects.
>
> *Dr. Caldwell Esselstyn*
> *Prevent and Reverse Heart Disease*

Reversing bodily health conditions that are products of how we Eat, Think and Live, may require letting go social customs established by commercialism in the blame-fear-hostility culture, plus clearing out old thought-emotional content still driving the boat. Taking a couple of weeks at a Cleansing, Detox, Nutritional and Mind-changing program can help ground new habits *(check our website)*. Developing consistency at home with New shopping list, food and recipes establishes good routines. Clearing old habitual thought patterns from conscious-unconscious Mind is necessary also to clearly invoke new habits

> When it comes to food choices, habit is stupendously powerful. Our familiar foods give us comfort, reassurance, and a sense of identity. They are there for us when the world may not be... On the other hand, it does take effort to question whether our conventional ways of thinking and acting truly serve us.
>
> *John Robbins*
> *Diet for a New America*

30

Time-honored instruction on "our ideal nutrition" is vegan fare though later instruction revolved around that people *were* consuming meat, most likely after survival of an ice age.

> Then God said, "I give you every seed-bearing plant on the face of the whole earth and every tree that has fruit with seed in it. They will be yours for food.
>
> *Genesis 1:29*

Another physician offering tremendous model for prevention and longevity, Dr. Neal Barnard, recommends low-fat vegan diet for maintenance of good health and reversal of heart dis-ease and diabetes. He is currently doing research to demonstrate that this regimen also reverses cancer. Dr. Barnard is founding president of the Physicians Committee for Responsible Medicine, an international network of physicians, scientists, and laypeople promoting preventive medicine.

> In my own Life, I decided to leave meat off my plate in medical school, but was a bit slow to realize dairy products and eggs are not health foods either.
>
> *Dr. Neal Barnard*
> *Get Healthy, Go Vegan Cookbook*

Dr. Barnard's advocacy of a low-fat, whole food, plant-based diet is presented for anyone to follow in his 15+ books that have sold over 2 million copies, including *Power Foods for the Brain* (prevention for Alzheimer's); *The 21-Day Weight Loss Kickstart*; *Dr. Neal Barnard's Program for Reversing Diabetes* (remove animal products; minimize vegetable oils, stick to low glycemic index); *Breaking the Food Seduction*. His *Get Healthy, Go Vegan Cookbook* and *Foods that Cause You to Lose Weight* have great recipes to help any of us get started, get inspired and change our Lives forever!

Dean Ornish says about Barnard, "[He is] a leading pioneer in educating the public about the healing power of diet and nutrition." Dr. Henry Heimlich (of the Heimlich maneuver and progressive treatments for malaria) says, "Barnard's tremendous influence on dietary practices and promotion of a vegan diet is done with such eloquence as to make the proposition sound almost inviting."

> We help people to begin truly healthful diets, and it is absolutely wonderful to see not only their success, but also their delight at their ability to break old habits and feel really healthy for a change.
>
> *Dr. Neal Barnard*
> *The 21-Day Weight Loss Kickstart*

Another landmark study was done by Dr. Colin Campbell, over 20 years with 3,700 adults in 65 counties in China. Dr. Campbell was professor of nutritional biochemistry at Cornell. He went to the China Study as top protein researcher and came back vegetarian.

His book, *The China Study: The Most Comprehensive Study of Nutrition Ever Conducted And the Startling Implications for Diet, Weight Loss, And Long-term Health*, has sold over 500,000 copies; reporting that all degenerative conditions are prevented and reversed with a mostly vegetarian whole foods diet (max 7% animal products). This book is bound to have long range ramifications and huge impact on our "scientific proof oriented" society. Here's what is being said about *The China Study*:

> Today AICR [American Institute for Cancer Research] advocates a predominantly plant-based diet for lower cancer risk because of the great work of Dr. Campbell and a few other visionaries, beginning around 25 years ago.
>
> *Marilyn Gentry*
> *President, AICR*

> [These] findings from the most comprehensive large study ever undertaken on relationship between diet and risk of developing dis-ease, are challenging much of American dietary dogma.
>
> *New York Times*

> The most important book on health, diet and nutrition ever written. Its impact will only grow over time and it will ultimately improve the health and longevity of tens of millions of people around the world.
>
> *John Mackey, CEO Whole Foods*

> This is one of the most important books about nutrition ever written—reading it may save your Life.
>
> *Dean Ornish, MD*
> *Dr. Dean Ornish's Program for Reversing Heart Dis-Ease*

Another vegan advocate, John Robbins, groomed as heir to the Baskin and Robbins family ice cream business, chose to walk away from Baskin-Robbins and immense wealth it represented to "...pursue the deeper American Dream, ...of a society at peace with its conscience because it respects and lives in harmony with all Life forms...a society that is truly healthy, practicing wise and compassionate stewardship of a balanced ecosystem."

> Few of us are aware that the act of eating can be a powerful statement of commitment to our own well-being, and at the same time the creation of a healthier habitat. Your health, happiness, and the future of Life on earth are rarely so much in your own hands as when you sit down to eat.
>
> *John Robbins*
> *Diet for a New America*

John Robbins became aware at a young age of the devastating effects of animal-based diet on humans, animals and the eco-system. He became a vegan activist and thought-leader with numerous best-selling books that offer a wealth of information about better food choices: *Voices of the Food Revolution, No Happy Cows, Diet for a new America*, and more. John is Founder of EarthSave International, co-founder and co-host 100,000+ member Food Revolution Network *foodrevolution.org*. Books also include *THE new GOOD Life: Living Better Than Ever in an Age of Less; HEALTHY AT 100: Scientifically Proven Secrets of the World's Healthiest and Longest-Lived Peoples; THE AWAKENED HEART: Meditations on Finding Harmony in a Changing World; RECLAIMING OUR HEALTH: Exploding Medical Myth.*

John Robbins' Life along with wife Deo and son Ocean, has been dedicated to living wisely on Planet Earth. His widespread impact resulting from a Life well-lived, is an example of walking away from societal promises of safety and security, and dedicating Life and talents to Heart-inspired Vision and Purpose. *Wow!*

> When I walked away from Baskin-Robbins and the money it represented, I did so because I knew there was a deeper dream. I did it because I knew that with all the reasons that each of us has to despair and become cynical, there still beats in our common heart our deepest prayers for a better Life and a more loving world.
>
> *John Robbins*
> *Diet for a New America*

I (Cary) was privileged to work with John Robbins, his family and co-author Jia Patton for a short time in Santa Cruz, California in early 1990s, which was inspirational and heartwarming. His work has been subject of cover stories and feature articles in San Francisco Chronicle, Los Angeles Times, Chicago Life, Washington Post and New York Times. His Life and work have also been featured in PBS special, *Diet For A new America*.

> You see the changes in many places. You see people refusing to buy shampoos or other body care products from companies that test on animals, and instead buying cosmetics and other household products that are made without cruelty. We're learning to see what we didn't see before, and then, when we have the courage, creating the changes that make our lives congruent with what we know.
>
> *John Robbins*
> *Healthy at 100*

John Robbins work in *Diet For A new America* brought to the forefront, how inhumane and environmentally damaging commercial animal food production is. Most factory farming practices are unbelievably horrendously destructive to Life, with animals injuriously imprisoned, piled on top of one another, rarely getting a minute of "real" Life.

> Animals do not 'give' their life to us, as the sugar-coated lie would have it. No, we take their lives. They struggle and fight to the last breath, just as we would do if we were in their place.
>
> *John Robbins*

If it is an individual's choice to consume meat, it is one thing to find a local producer who is raising animals organically and humanely, and another to just pick up a neatly wrapped package in the meat department at your grocery store, with little thought as to what that animal went through in its Life for that package of meat to be there in your hands. It's essential we wake up to the implications of our actions. Pigs are the 4th most intelligent animal known, and what most know them for is bacon or ham. Devastating.

Rather than closed eyes, do your research, watch films, visit animal food production, and then consider vegan or vegetarianism. Watch: *Fast food Nation, Supersize Me* and *Forks*

Over Knives, others recommended by PETA (people for ethical treatment of animals). Respect Universal Law, use Mind-Energy and choose your Vibration wisely.

> Once you start to notice the surging interest in compassion toward animals, you find it's everywhere...
>
> Although extreme crowding of animals greatly increases rates of animals' illness and death, it nevertheless also raises profits. Even when more than 20 percent of pigs and chickens die prematurely in today's intensive husbandry systems for instance, producers find their profits increased by such practices.
>
> Overcrowding that's typical today would once have been unthinkable, because animals kept in such conditions would have been decimated by dis-ease. Now, with antibiotics mixed into every meal, with widespread use of hormones, drugs, and biocides, enough animals are kept alive so overcrowding becomes cost-effective...
>
> Layer hens, meanwhile, are crammed together in cages so tiny that they do not have enough space even to begin to lift a single wing...More than 99 percent of the hens who lay eggs eaten in the United States are debeaked and kept in cages where the excrement from the birds in the upper tiers collects above them, often falling through onto their heads.'

John Robbins
Diet for a new America

It's easy to say, "Oh these choices would be difficult to make because of my husband, wife, family, or what my neighbors and friends might think," or "I might have to learn something New." Or if you're a confirmed meat, egg and dairy eater, one good option is to find a humane local producer, and buy from them rather than abusive mass production. And yes, this kind of awareness may stimulate changes, yet it can also be easy and fun. As we continue to develop Mastery, such food choices become a matter of Awareness.

> There are people in the world so hungry,
> that God cannot appear to them except in the form of bread.

Mahatma Gandhi (1969-1948)
Non-Violent Leader of India

Outside health of our body, and health and welfare of hundreds of millions of animals suffering today, the ecology of our Planet is also at stake. New York Times Week In Review reported in Jan. 2008, "Rethinking the Meat Guzzler," "Just this week, the president of Brazil announced emergency measures to halt burning and cutting of rain forest for crop-grazing land [by such as McDonalds]. In the last five months alone, the government says, 1,250 square miles were lost."

> ...The real cause of hunger is a scarcity of justice, not a scarcity of food. Enough grain is squandered every day in raising American livestock for meat to provide every human being on earth with two loaves of bread.

John Robbins, Diet for a new America:
How Your Food Choices Affect Your Health,
Happiness and the Future of Life on Earth

This is a Mind-full to consider. If you are not vegan or vegetarian, there is wisdom in considering this "path" for your body, the environment and all creatures. Daniel of the Old Testament and his men, on a diet of "pulse" (peas and beans) were "fairer and fatter than all the kings men." If you are of the mindset that you *must have* animal products, accessing those produced in a humane manner, to bring a different kind of resonance through you.

> The ancient Greeks told of a philosopher eating bread and lentils for dinner. He was approached by another man, who lived sumptuously by flattering the king. Said the flatterer, "If you would learn to be subservient to the king, you would not have to live on lentils." The philosopher replied, "If you would learn to live on lentils, you would not have to give up your independence in order to be docile and acquiescent to the king.

> *John Robbins*
> *The new Good Life: Living Better Than Ever in an Age of Less*

Teddi suggests to her clients, "Only eat it if it's a whole food, not processed and picked as it grew." Cary's philosophy has been, *"Whole foods in as close to their simple and natural form as possible."* Cary's book **Super Immunity Secrets,** available on Amazon and Kindle, is a great guide, with 50 easy basic everyday vegan-vegetarian recipes, belongs in every kitchen *(check our website).* Also look for Food Prep videos at our website and Youtube.

One of the most empowering solutions to many issues we face today includes growing a garden, or buying from local growers. One man in Los Angeles featured on TED startted "Guerrilla Gardens" on median strips and any open soil in L.A., giving birth to neighborhood access to free fresh food. Barbara Kingsolver's *Animal, Vegetable, Miracle: A Year of Food Life,* is a wonderful story of a family who ate only what was obtainable locally for a year! inspirational! Another family lived *Trash Free* for a Year, blogging about this New way to Live, ending up with only one tiny ziplock of trash at the end! We can do it!

A clean body supports clear Mind-Energy. Now popular Raw Food movement and Juicing, cleanses, alkalizes and brings the Body into harmonious function; it is easier than ever to get on a "cleanup program." Enzymes and Life-force of Raw-Living Foods-Juices restore Life-giving elements to cells. Dr. Gabriel Cousens, MD author of *Conscious Eating,* who established Tree of Life rejuvenation and learning center near Patagonia, Arizona says:

> A live-food diet has been used with great success to heal...degenerative dis-eases or poor states of health, such as arthritis, high blood pressure, menstrual difficulties, obesity, allergies, diabetes, ulcers, heart and other circulatory dis-eases, hormone disturbances, diverticulosis, anemia, weak immune system, and other poor states of health. Many people have found a live-food diet an excellent aid for improving brain/mind function...a high percentage of live food in the diet plays an important part in creating healthful longevity.

So is there a black-and-white answer as to what is the best *live-it* or *die-it?* The truth is, we choose our food based on where we are in Awareness. As we clear unconscious content, live in the Heart and focus in LOVE, we are most likely moving toward Lighter, rejuvenating, kind, organic nutrition and Lifestyle, based around *ahimsa,* ancient practice of harmlessness. Honor others' choices, Live with Joy on your own path.

> It seems the whole works of humankind are backwards. Most are trying to convince, instruct, and purify everyone else - without first purifying themselves. To enlighten others we have to enlighten ourselves.
>
> David Wolfe
Sunfood Diet Success System

Whatever our choices, it's important to Live without judgment. The the more present we are, the more clear it becomes how we affect the whole. The more Awake we are, the more we consider every action to be an act of consciousness, ruled by the Universal Law of Cause and Affect. Becoming vegan or vegetarian, obtaining our food in ecological holistic ways emanates from the Heart. As "fear-hostility" clear from our Vibration we naturally shift to kinder choices. Everything that manifests is a result of Vibrational cause. Let go of fear about whatever you choose. The biggest cause to act from, is our True Design, LOVE.

> Vegetarianism preserves Life, health, peace and ecology, Creates a more equitable distribution of resources, helps feed the hungry, encourages nonviolence for animal and human members of the planet, and is a powerful aid for spiritual transformation of body, emotions, mind and spirit.
>
> Gabriel Cousens
Conscious Eating

Foods and beverages can be used as "drugs" to numb us. It may take choice of will to remove ourselves from surrounding temptations. It requires sincere dedication and effort to exit social inertia, and instead set ourselves up with nourishing food and beverages. Layers of belief systems we grew up with and cultural programming can be "sticky wickets" to move beyond. Be patient with the process, LOVE self and let go all judgment. Empower yourself with your deep Heart-felt Desire to Live with Health and Vibrancy.

Instead of doing battle with inner struggles, use our essential tools [Part 2: MIND], to clear resonance from the unconscious. Align with Universal Laws 1 & 3 Mind-Energy, Vibration. As we release and let go blame-fear-hostility, food choices naturally Lighten up.

Deepening Heart connection we find our way, discovering we Know that we Know, based on Eternal connection with the Innate. We enter a chrysalis like the caterpillar, unwinding the old paradigm through deep transformative darkness and chaos of Mirrored shadows, emerging finally into our True Design LOVE, stretching our New wings to fly.

> This genius is inside you, a part of your inner blueprint that cannot be erased..."The inner intelligence of the body is the ultimate and supreme genius in nature. It mirrors the wisdom of the cosmos." (Vedic text)... At the Quantum mechanical level, there is no sharp boundary dividing you from the rest of the Universe.
>
> Deepak Chopra M
Perfect Health: A Complete Mind-Body Guide

Frequencies of foods below measured with a radionics machine demonstrate how much they raised body vitality. Those at top #1 raised it most. This basic awareness of energies and frequencies of foods was mapped by Margueritte Weippers, who used radionics to consistently grow incredibly extraordinary organic blueberries.

ELECTROVIBRATORY RATE OF NOURISHMENT OF FOODS

1. Chelated Colloidal Mineral Water
2. Fresh Pressed Greens - Wheatgrass, Spirulina, Chlorella
3. Sprouts
4. Fresh Pressed Fruits & Vegetables (juiced or blended)
5. Raw Salads
6. Raw Fruits
7. Sprouted Seeds and Nuts
8. Sprouted Grains - Essene Bread
9. Highly Mineralized Herbs
10. Bee Pollen
11. Raw Honey

1. Legumes cooked with spices
2. Seeds & Nuts (ground and soaked)
3. Steamed Veggies
4. Baked Potatoes or Yams
5. Brown Rice and Whole Grains, cooked
6. Natural Sweet Treats - carob, seeds, fruit, raw honey

Do not live in the body alone; live in consciousness. Be aware of your progress. Know your destiny. Meaning will become clear. Seek gratefully, ask reverently...knock humbly. And above all have faith, you will receive!

Margueritte Weippers
Radionics Master

NUTRITION LEVELS LIST

Use upper 3 categories below to "Lighten up." A common option is to cleanse one day per week and have a salad daily, it depends on you. Variety is important. Listen to YOUR body & intuition; get organic-naturally grown, local whenever possible.

CLEANSING

Fasting - water, fresh air, sunshine, gentle movement, Breathing, rest

Beverages - water; water with lemon, herbal tea, pinch baking soda

Juices - fresh only, dilute with water 1/5th - excellent for cleansing & nourishing

Cleanses - (homemade or purchased) eliminative herbs, psyllium, flax

REGENERATIVE - ALL RAW

Green Shakes /Smoothies water /vegan milk, fruit fresh-frozen, green powders, algae, grasses, seaweeds, superfoods, soaked seeds & nuts, hemp, flax, greens

Fruits - ripe, in season, eat only with light foods for best digestion

Veggies- ripe, in season - raw in salads

Sprouts - alfalfa, clover, radish, broccoli, peas, adzuki beans, mung, sunnies

Fermented Foods - raw: sauerkraut, kimchee, rejuvelac

Nuts and Seeds - soaked overnight, then refrigerate

Dried Fruit (no sulphur or sugar) rehydrated

Essene Bread - sprouted grains - very low temp or dehydrate

Seasonings - Herbs, Spices. Lemon, sm. amt. olive/coconut oil, cayenne, Celtic, Himalayan or sea salt, dulse & seaweeds, garlic, onion, nutritional yeast

MAINTENANCE - COOKED VEGAN *(recipes at our website)*

Fruits - ripe, in season, (separate from veggies) raw or simple pies/jams

Veggies- baked, steamed, sautéed

Soups - veggies, moderate grains, beans, herbs

Legumes - soak 12-24 hrs, pour off water, sprout and/or simmer

Grains - lean toward non-gluten such as rice, quinoa, amaranth, oats

Nuts & Seeds, Nut Butters - great oil source, whole raw, not sprouted

Ezekiel or Essene Sprouted Grain Bread - sprouted grains, seeds, veggies

Whole Grain Preparations (sprouted preferred) tortillas, bread, crackers, pasta

Seasoning - see list above

LACTO-OVO VEGETARIAN All of above plus Healthy, Organic, Humanely, Kindly Farm Produced Eggs & Dairy. Generous foods from all previous categories

FISH - MEAT Reduce quantity, organic, have less often, obtain only humanely raised, increase foods from all above categories. HUMANE CARE: Temple Grandin's work listed in *Time's 100 Most Influential People: Heroes*, documentary "The Woman Who Thinks Like A Cow." *"Nature is cruel but we don't have to be; we owe them some respect."*

REMOVE White flour, white sugar, excesses, processed, fast and fried foods

GREAT RECIPES - Cary's book, ***Super Immunity Secrets,*** quick, easy, delicious, vegan-vegetarian w/shopping list. *(See our website for more books and videos)*

Climb the Transitional Ladder Chart chart by Cary Ellis. *(check our website)*

FOOD FOR THOUGHT: Mind-Energy covers *everything:* we may seek health due to our of fear of death. Or we may say, "Live for today," and do whatever we feel like. As we let go fear, clearing unconscious content, we choose to be healthy, embracing Life. Genetic patterns often trigger food choices. These shift as we clear our unconscious data and integrate Higher Frequency dynamics, from choice point of Now. *Choosing a healthy path requires dedication and commitment, yet bears fruit in results that uplift the entire Life.*

CAUSE & EFFECT Universal Law: How does this work with food? Just ask yourself, "Did this food come from the Earth Mother, in a natural wholesome form, in Vibrational harmony and Coherence with my body?" If the answer is Yes, then enjoy it with LOVE and Gratitude. If its production is based on refinement or suffering to get it to your table, seek other choices and consider *effect* manifested from *cause.* [*Universal Laws Part 2: MIND*]

> So the question that remains is: Why does the live-food diet give us the best effect in terms of decreasing our caloric intake and maximizing the quality of our food intake? The point from basic nutrient mathematics is that by eating live foods, we get complete nutrition by eating 50 to 80 percent less food.
>
> *Dr. Gabriel Cousens*
> *Spiritual Nutrition*

WEIGHT LOSS AND HEALTHY WEIGHT MAINTENANCE: Many yo-yo with dietary confusion. The most vital solution is to remove all animal products and refined foods; follow *Daily Cleansing: Simple Rules* in our *Cleanse and Detox* chapter. Find Cary's books at Amazon: *Why Become a Vegetarian?* and *Truth About Weight Loss* and more at our website.

DAILY REGENERATIVE REGIMEN

Adapt and apply to what fits for you! (visit our website for more)

These Lifestyle Habits bring Vitality and Clarity to our Mind-Energy. Masters of all ages have harmonized body and spirit with simple high-frequency nourishment. RULES: 4-5 hrs. btw. meals; 12 hrs. at night empty stomach; moderate meal size. Choose from suggested foods suitable to your path.

UPON ARISING

❏ Stretch, Breathe, notice what is bubbling up, note dreams, or "worries" to clear with quick goal canceling or tapping - give them to the *Field.* (see Part 2: MIND)

❏ You are rising from fasting all night. Honor this - rooted in the 5th Universal Law (Mutable) of Rhythm. During morning routine, to flush elimination from night's fast from cells, organs, tissues, DRINK *1 quart warm:*
   • water or water water with a wedge of lemon or lime
   • or water with lemon-lime and a pinch of baking soda *(alkalizing)*
   • herbal tea *(no caffeine for cleansing, then regular tea or coffee after)*

❏ **GREEN SHAKE** Pre mixed green powder or Create your own combo *including*: grass powders, chlorella, Spirulina, blue-green algae, golden flax (ground-soaked), fresh or frozen fruit, water, nut-seed milk, vegan protein powder, chia, hemp

❏ **BREAKFAST** - The Lighter we become, the more the above is sufficient. For more, let the above settle then have your choice from list

- Smoothies, Raw nuts, Fruit
- Ezekiel or Essene bread-toast, plain, w/nut butter (opt.)
- Muesli cereal raw - oats, nuts, dried fruit - soaked overnight
- Potatoes, tofu, toast, or *choice of above list based on current Lifestyle*

☐ **LUNCH** - drink water or beverage on empty stomach 1/2 hr before meal
- Raw salad, veggies, sprouts, sprouted seeds, dress with All Raw Seasonings list above. Once a habit these become good craving!
- Sandwich or roll up made with sprouts, veggies (your pick on list above)
- Ezekiel or Essene bread-toast, plain, w/nut butter (opt.)
- Cooked veggies or Soup (homemade when possible - make on weekend to have during week)
- If animal products desired: *quantity size of palm of hand*

☐ **DINNER** - drink beverages on empty stomach 1/2 hr before meal
- Raw salad, veggies, sprouts, sprouted seeds, dress with All Raw Seasonings list above. Once a habit salads become a good craving!
- Ezekiel or Essene bread-toast, plain, w/nut butter (opt.)
- Cooked, baked, steamed veggies
- Soup - one of our mainstays - especially in chilly weather, a great Light, hearty nourishment with veggies, herbs, spices, a little grain, legume - so easy to prepare - throw everything in pot and let simmer when home to have later in week if it lasts!
- If you desire animal products, *quantity size of palm of hand*

> It's not what goes into your mouth that defiles you;
> you are defiled by the words that come out of your mouth.
>
> *Matthew 15:11*

Mind-Energy or Vibration within us calls Creation into being, thus determining the state of our physical body and our "reality." Establishing LOVING family and community we find support for better choices, as "no one is an island." Joining others who share Visions and Dreams carries us a long way toward well-being. *[Part 3: SPIRIT]*

Over the years we have followed healthy lifestyle practices, both Teddi and I (Cary) have found our own paths become simpler and simpler. We have learned to have a deep gratitude for that which is given us, as Sun Bear taught, and to encompass the prayer that all may be fed, and we may give our Lives to service that brings well-being to ALL.

After breathing, we smile...Contemplating our food for a few seconds before eating, and eating in mindfulness, can bring us much happiness...Having the opportunity to sit with family and friends and enjoy wonderful food is something precious, something not everyone has. Many people in the world are hungry. When I hold a bowl of rice or a piece of bread, I know that I am fortunate, and I feel compassion for all those who have no food to eat and are without friends or family. This is a very deep practice...Mindful eating can cultivate seeds of compassion and understanding that will strengthen us to do something to help hungry and lonely people to be nourished.

John Robbins
Diet for a New World

CARY'S LIFESTYLE JOURNEY: I was lucky enough to grow up in the midst of gardens and an orchard, with wonderful produce that fed us and others all year. Our Mediterranean diet with small amounts of meat and abundant fruit and vegetables was quite healthy. I went to the West Coast from Michigan at age 18, where my World opened up to new ideas including becoming vegetarian.

So for 40+ years I have been various forms of vegan, vegetarian, occasionally a tiny bit of fish or dairy, with longest periods on mostly Raw and Living Foods. My current Lifestyle is 65%-95% Raw depending upon season, location, availability; Green Shakes, salads, herbs, spices, juice, Essene or Ezekiel bread, nuts, seeds, legumes, quinoa, amaranth or rice mostly in winter soups and salads. Simple. Simple.

I met Teddi with her then husband Lou in 1980, when they visited the Wheatgrass Institute in Michigan where I was co-director. This center was a most significant and enjoyable experience of my Life: great community, crew, gardens, and many attendees learning to Live Lifestyle-changes. Consuming large amounts of wheatgrass juice, sprouting, fasting, cleansing, juices, banquets of Living food, Life supporting rejuvenation. I encourage anyone seeking higher levels of Vitality to experience such an immersion in cleansing and high frequency nutrition to accelerate your Journey.

EVERYTHING we share here is a result of having seen thousands of lives change over many years. We have both always sought simple, practical, effective answers that individuals can carry out themselves. Being Healthy is not complicated, yet takes re-education. It is easy to feel like you're stuck, or to think you can't do it, yet the reason we are here with you is because we LOVE what we're doing and know you can change too. It's easier than you think, and we're here to guide you!

Much on this journey of Life inspired me to question more deeply, such as being around hunting and extreme winters in the Colorado Rocky Mountains for 16 years; deciding whether to feed my dogs meat and when they died of cancer, questioning whether they really were carnivorous, wishing I'd been knowledgeable enough not to vaccinate; watching many friends who had been vegetarian go back to meat eating; watching some people die of cancer and other degenerative conditions and others get well, always seeking to know why. Reflecting on my own experiences of Mind-Energy and Body, I've always searched for answers to such deep and probing questions.

41

My sweetest discoveries revolve around how physical health is a result of so much more than physical habits. I flow more Freely these days, with simple gratitude for what IS, knowing many in the World do not currently have choices available that I do. My Life is dedicated to practical solutions now on a Globally scale, initiating a New Civilization based in LOVE. Most important for me these days, is following my Heart of Hearts to Live Authentically from Essence... ♥ *Cary*

TEDDI'S LIFESTYLE JOURNEY: *As a child I had a natural aversion to dairy products. My parents couldn't get me to eat an egg, even if they disguised it or scrambled it. And as for anything like meat, beef or chicken, if I saw the bones, that was it for me! I am so thankful that my parents gave me the opportunity to choose what my Body-Mind-Spirit told me to eat!*

So you might ask, why was a child like me so filled with food dislikes? The one answer is this, my grandfather lived on a farm a few miles from our house... and we visited often. So I knew what the barn and the chicken coop smelled like. Milk came into our house warm and smelled like the cows, eggs came into our house dirty and had to be cleaned or sandpapered before they were put into the fridge. Because I was brought up with a truck farm nearby, and we had large gardens, I always knew there was plenty of food to choose from and unlimited fresh fruit and vegetables, making healthy food choices easy.

Needless to say when I had my four children, I listened to their individual choices. I continue to know that gardening is a way of Life for me wherever I am. I am fully aware of the Food Pyramids, the Whole Foods Ladder, the Maker's Diet, Eating Right for Your Blood Type, and the list goes on and on, and still I like the gentle "middle path," based in a variety of good, natural, organic, unprocessed, fresh and simply prepared whole foods..

Thirty years of client services working directly with Dr. Stone's environmentally sensitive clients and nutritional soundness with Dr. Versendaal, gave me depth of insight on advice focused around individual needs, which I have come to understand is ultimately important. Reminding people to listen to their own intuition and get to know their body offers a primary key to wellness.

I have had a simple approach to living healthfully. I listen to my body. I make good natural, whole food choices, and I leave a little wiggle room for picnics, parties and play. Do your best to keep fear out of your food or the food of others; bless what you do have, and eat as close to nature as possible. ♥ *Teddi*

Chapter 4

Superior Supplements: *Superfoods*

Superfoods represent a uniquely promising piece of the nutrition puzzle, as they are great sources of clean protein, vitamins, minerals, enzymes, antioxidants, good fats and oils, nutrients, essential fatty and amino acids.

David Wolfe
Superfoods: The Food and Medicine of the Future

Our favorite way of buffing-out nutrition, providing the Body "super" nutrients on which to thrive, is with powerful whole "Superfoods," the most nutrient dense foods on the Planet. They increase vital force, boost the immune system, elevate serotonin production, enhance sexuality and alkalize. Mother Nature contains within her bounty an amazing array of super-nutrients not found in your local grocery store. Our first LOVE of Superfoods is grasses, algae and other greens.

We consider them *Essential* to high-quality nutrition.

Many Superfoods have been used in Ancient cultures for thousands of years, to promote longevity and vitality. Incorporating Superfoods into our Lifestyle may take a little research, as some are shipped from faraway, though Now so popular, many can be easily ordered online or purchased at your local health food store.

Once you become involved in the Superfoods "community" you are likely to meet interesting people, and change your Life as a result. Superfoods tap us into Ancient roots of natural Wisdom, activating latent elements in our consciousness. They carry in their cellular memory millennia of "plant knowing" and Living elements. Viewed with Kirlian photography superfoods have large vibrant, radiant auras, electromagnetic or pranic *Fields*. This super vital Life force is transmitted to us, as we use them with LOVE and Gratitude.

In ancient Egypt green was used for healing, and this has proves itself out over and over through various programs. Powerful foods for regeneration are grasses and algae. Observing the regenerative condition of people in our circles over many years, daily consumption of these foods seems to make the biggest difference. When I (Cary) look around at other people my age and I ask myself the difference between them and what I have done for so long, my conclusion has been that daily for 40 over years I have consumed a green shake of some sort or green drinks with grasses, living green leaves and algae for protein consistently.

Participating in wheatgrass and living foods institutes proved this out, watching hundreds of people transform their bodies in just a manner of weeks. Also, working with Gerson Cancer Therapy Institute where 13 juices per day produced amazing results.

I have been in dialogue with close friend Dennis since early 1980s, who consistently included endurance in his regimens. He participated in numerous hundred mile ultramarathons, through-hiked Appalachian Trail in five months, and over many years has consistently been a high-level athlete as a mostly Raw Vegan - Vegetarian, and "O" blood type.

At the time of this writing he is 70 years young, and one of the most vital bright people I know. He and his wife Wendy live authentic, "present" lives filled with the kind of vitality most people dream of yet think may be out of reach. They would like others to know this is attainable, though requires commitment to Lifestyle changes. One of their secrets to operating at this level of well-being is dedication to expressing True *Essence,* Living for the betterment for humanity and participating in service to others.

> To me conscious living means I'm aware of each and everything that I do in terms of my thoughts, what I put into my body and the ways I keep my body fit and whole. This translates into how I make choices about everything I think, say and do.
>
> *Dennis Shackley*
> *Leader The Mankind Project, Raw Food Vegan*

In a culture where a majority have long been caught in poor nutritional practices, it's awesome to have a circle of friends modeling excellence, as this is how we learn and grow, by associating with others dedicated to Mastery. In our ongoing dialogs with one another Dennis and I have concluded, observing our lives, that consistency with grasses, greens and algae, with salads and other Raw foods, is an *essential* piece that has helped us both stay consistently vital and regenerative. This is a Life-path commitment! What Dennis and I would like others to know, is that this is within reach for ANYONE. It simply requires dedication to get and stay on the path of Awakened Living.

There is Now a cultural wave going on, including younger generations and and all ages getting into juicing and raw foods. This is very exciting! When a person cultivates desire, they can also find companionship, inspiration, support and community. We acknowledge friendships over many years, are one of biggest support for each of us to stay with our chosen path, with dialogue, encouragement, and space held without judgement to look deeper into unraveling our own shadows. The Buddy System works! Find friends and community of matching Vibration to inspire you to live *Lightly* today*!*

We find the most regenerative *Live-it* foods are concentrated green powders containing grasses and algae along with fresh greens such as kale or spinach and more. Moving away from traditional Lifestyle, using greens daily is a big habit to incorporate. This single simple habit heightens our potential for well-being and vitality, and gets us on a track for revitalized living. Daily greens keep us resilient, chase away illness, with clarity of Mind-Energy, higher Vibrational frequency and positive effect on the Whole. Change yourself, change the World. *Arc the Hologram Now with LOVE!*

Concentrated Green Superfoods

Most below are available at local health food store or ordered easily online. Wheatgrass is easy and inexpensive to grow at home. Some adventurous Souls are learning aquaculture to grow algae, very exciting as Dr. Christopher Hills taught that we could completely feed ALL with this single regenerative food. These are some of the most basic and concentrated foods on the Planet, best to be enjoyed in shakes or can alternatively be taken in capsules or bars on the go.

WHEATGRASS & BARLEY GRASS [grasses of grains gluten free at this stage of development] harvested within first 7-14 days are a rich chlorophyll source, very alkalizing, aid in cell detoxification, internal cleansing, cleanse and rebuild, improv energy and mental clarity by oxygenating blood, improve digestion, contain concentrated nutrients, iron, calcium, magnesium, amino acids, vitamins A, C, K, E; are 22% protein. Grasses are potent antioxidants, reducing Body stress by neutralizing toxins. Grass powder is good, *juice powder* is even more potent and excellent to use on a daily basis!

ORMUS SUPERGREENS by Sunwarrior are grown in volcanic soil; highly mineralized it is loaded with micro amounts of platinum, gold and silver. These ORMUS trace minerals instill the greens with a magnetic Life force property, raising Vibrational frequency for those consuming it. Use of such potent greens can activate higher energetic frequencies in the Body, so better to increase slowly with this Ancient Alchemy. *Ormus Supergreens* also contain oat grass, barley and wheatgrass alfalfa, yucca, stevia parsley, spinach, probiotic, peppermint.

SPIRULINA an algae, is 60% complete protein and contains important vitamins and minerals, B complex, vitamin E, carotenoids, iodine, iron, manganese, zinc, essential fatty acids such as gamma-Linolenic acid (found in mother's milk), more beta carotene than carrots! Plant source B12.

CHLORELLA is high in chlorophyll. Raw, broken-cell walled chlorella is deep green in color, is considered to enhance immune system, increases growth of "friendly" bacteria, lowers blood pressure and cholesterol, promotes healing of intestinal issues, "cleanses" blood and liver; is protective against cancer, diabetes and other degenerative conditions. Chlorella attracts and cleanse the Body of toxins and heavy metals; it is particularly useful in clearing mercury exposure commonly resulting from old dental fillings and coal burning power plants.

BLUE-GREEN ALGAE Algae first appeared on the planet over 3.5 billion years ago. As one of the first Life forms capable of photosynthesis, it quickly became a primary foundation food for all Life on the planet. During photosynthesis, sunlight transforms water and carbon dioxide in algae into oxygen, essential nutrients, elemental compounds and vibrant Life-energy. As a result, algae is responsible for an astonishing 80% of the global oxygen supply and provides vital nourishment for every species that consumes it. It is a valuable phytonutrient considered by many to be one of nature's most cleansing and regenerating substances.

It provides a highly bioavailable protein that is 80% assimilated in our bodies (compared to meat protein, which is only 20% assimilated). Blue-green algae's amino acid profile is optimal for humans; and it contains the world's most concentrated source of chlorophyll.

The Toltec, Aztec and Mayan Indians so prized algae for its powerful, Life-sustaining qualities that they cultivated it in carefully built aqueducts. The Kanembu people of Saharan Africa continue the ancient tradition of annual pilgrimages to Lake Johann to gather the vital wild algae blooming in its waters for nourishment and food throughout the coming year. Today, scientific research has confirmed what traditional cultures always knew - algae is one of the most nutrient-dense and restorative whole foods available to humankind. Many scientists and nutritionists expect the extraordinary properties of edible algae to play a substantial role in feeding and healing people of the 21st century.

GREEN POWDER BLENDS - Many awesome blends are now available that containing greens to seaweed, mushrooms and high frequency superfoods. One of these is a great way to get started, rather than multiple bags or bottles. There are only four or five different organizations that actually make greens Blends so what you will start noticing Read labels and you will learn to recognize the various blends, try them out and discover which you like best.

There are numerous excellent resources online and at your local health food store to obtain these items; try a few things till you become familiar with what works for you and what you like. It's always good when starting out with concentrated green powders, to start with a small amount such as 1/4 teaspoon of each, gradually increase, as they can initiate cleansing. Gradually increase to larger amounts, blending them into green shakes every morning; so nutritious these are sustaining for much of the day. Using a mix of grasses and algae it is amazing how well nutritional needs are met with added protein of the algae; we find these green shakes a mainstay.

> When you are young and healthy, it never occurs to you
> that in a single second your whole Life could change.
>
> *Annette Funicello (1942-2013)*
> *Actress, Singer, Mouseketeer*

We have seen much recovery from dis-ease and access to wellness over many years, by those committed to transforming their Lives with these concentrated green Superfoods, clearly showing their value. While running the wheatgrass institute one man with leukemia who had a blood count so low he should have been dead, after using wheatgrass juice for one week achieved a normal blood count. Composition of hemoglobin and chlorophyll are identical except hemoglobin has iron at its nucleus and and chlorophyll has magnesium. As a result chlorophyll rebuilds the blood and tissues very quickly.

> To keep the body in good health is a duty...
> otherwise we shall not be able to keep our mind strong and clear.
>
> *Buddha*

I (Cary) observed a client at Gerson Cancer Institute eliminate a grapefruit-sized tumor through his chest wall. This is the power of aligning with Life in *harmony* with nature, clearing Mind and Heart. This is the power of rightly lived Cause and Effect, resulting in manifestation transforming from the inside out. To accomplish such required commitment to grow beyond societal and personal conditioning. This is an elite visionary, who recognized the value of regenerative Lifestyle to sustain, maintain, regain optimum health and clarity of Body-Mind-Spirit. Superfoods hold a cellular dynamic that plays a key role in such recoveries, empowering restoration of a living clean vital body.

> The way you think, the way you behave,
> the way you eat, can influence your Life-span by 30 to 50 years.
>
> *Deepak Chopra MD*
> *Natural Physician, New Thought Author*

After a near-fatal car crash, Mitchell May was told he would never walk again. Thanks to his dedication to heal and support of his medically oriented family who went beyond their conditioning, he made medical history by regenerating nerve, bone, muscle and organ tissue, after his Body was almost totally crushed. On this extraordinary healing journey, he learned the art of non-traditional self-healing. He developed a powerful Superfood blend, *Pure Synergy*, which was all he consumed for a year, recovering use of bone, muscle and nerve thought beyond hope. Pure Synergy has since, offered healing Lifestyle to others.

> A wise man should consider that health is the greatest of human blessings, and
> learn how by his own thought to derive benefit from his illnesses.
>
> *Hippocrates (460 B.C.- 367 B.C.)*
> *Father of Modern Medicine*

These stories and more, assist us to realize it is never too late to heal, to make the choice to be well, to change the course or direction our Body is headed. It is always a choice of Mind-Heart based Action. The Body is an amazing miraculous mechanism, *whose pure drive is toward Life.* As we remove toxins blocking Life-force from poor habits, and provide high-frequency Superfoods, the body moves diligently toward wholeness and wellness. This is how we access brightness of Mind and Spirit and give our best to Life.

Many unhealthy Lifestyle habits are perpetuated when we suppress expression of Truth and Authenticity, or carry around pain that is a resonance we must remove from the unconscious. Utilizing tools in other parts of this series: Part 2: MIND and Part 3: SPIRIT, are essential for ultimate well-being, as Body-Mind-Spirit are infinitely connected.

Freeing ourselves from a false sense of obligation and duty developed in the blame-fear-hostility culture, and bringing forth the creative Being that Lives within us, vital Superfoods *accelerate* the process. Even working through a residual of old suppressive habits, adding Superfoods such as a green shake daily strengthens Mind and Heart to assist us in releasing these old cycles.

This is LOVING self. Superfood nutrition helps bring clarity to Mind and Heart to LOVE more and let go suppressive habits, because it feels so good to be clear! It provides clarity of Mind to bring inspired Dreams into being, strengthening us to courageously find the way on our own path of Living Authentically from *Essence.* Seeking to know and express the depths of who we are, is ultimately the driving force in finding peace.

Before we take a look at the more exotic Superfoods, let's dig a little deeper into why we're hungry for them, which returns us to lack of mineralization in declining soils. We *can* get Super-nutrients from organically grown produce in our back yards; however most soils are so depleted, nutrient value they ought to have is not there. If you are lucky enough to have garden rich soil, you're an "exclusive clubber," and you have one of the best foundations possible, deeply harmonious with Pachamama or Mother Earth. Adding rock dust to your garden soil is a huge bonus, to increase longevity and resistance to dis-ease.

Our immune system and even our physical structure, is a reflection of the foods we have eaten from either toxic and nutrient depleted soils, or wonderfully fertile soils.

Eryn Paige
How to Grow Glorious Wheatgrass at Home Tutorial - With Salty Sea Mineral Eco-Fertilization

If you are an avid organic gardener, you know that vegetables grown in your garden taste infinitely better than grocery store produce and are Worlds apart. In fact, delicious, sweet and "addicting" food grows in highly mineralized soils. This is why we have a natural hunger for sweetness, and why sweetness is addicting, because our bodies are looking for sweetness that is naturally occurring in foods grown in highly mineralized soil.

Our psychobiology *knows* highly mineralized foods are the best thing possible for us to consume. To optimally improve soil at home in your garden, obtain rock dust at your local gravel pit where rock is sorted, and incorporate it into your soil with humus, compost and other organic matter. This remineralization is essential, as we are about to learn. The land of the Hunzas in the Himalayas and Villacamba Valley in Ecuador, both are examples of highly mineralized soil from glacial runoff, boasting many centenarians.

> The soil is the great connector of lives, the source and destination of all. It is the healer and restorer and resurrector, by which dis-ease passes into health, age into youth, death into Life. Without proper care for it we can have no community, because without proper care for it we can have no Life.
>
> *Wendell Berry, Author, Farmer, Activist*
> *The Unsettling of America: Culture and Agriculture*

Mineralization is one of the most critical needs of our bodies, which must be supplied through organic plant matter or in fulvic (organic easy to absorb) form to be assimilated. We were at one time instrumental in discovering a rich source of fulvic minerals, which friends now distribute. We consider these a first line of defense for the body for superior mineralization, and will have a special offer for them at our website. First we can use such a resource to mineralize ourselves; next we'll look at how to mineralize the Planet.

Let's take a look at why mineralizing the soil with rock dust offers a critical key to our very survival. John D. Haymaker was a talented mechanical engineer, ecologist, and researcher in soil remineralization, rock dust, mineral cycles, climate cycles and glaciology. He made the important correlation that our global climate issues are a result of soil demineralization, and highly at cause in global warming. He came up with a brilliant plan to remineralize soil with rock dust, by mimicking what a glacier does, without us having to go through hundreds of years in an Ice Age to get the same results.

In 1982 Haymaker wrote an extremely important book in conjunction with California ecologist Donald A. Weaver, called *The Survival Of Civilization* (accessible free online); please pass it on into millions of hands. This work inspired a growing movement toward natural remineralization of soil. Findings were corroborated by scientists in the UK. Haymaker appeared on Ted Turner's Atlanta Superstation, and Scripps Institute of Oceanography. *Scientific American* also published articles backing his work.

Haymaker pointed out that we face the threat of an imminent ice age, and how this can be averted by remineralizing with rock dust and reforestation to restore $CO2$ levels by propagating "carbon sinks" (carbon lost through deforestation) for climatic stability, *which would result in two moderate seasons each year. How wonderful is this?*

Though Haymaker has departed this World, Don Weaver continues this important work with his latest book, *Regenerate the Earth*. These two became catalysts for the founding of a great organization, Remineralize The Earth, Now doing projects Worldwide. Besides mineralizing soils for better nutrition, they are using rock dust to bioremediate oil spills on farm lands and in waterways, restoring soil fertility and carbon sequestration. They are a great organization to volunteer with. Remineralize dot org Stepping out of "normal" routines to volunteer or participate in such work can help build a highly sustainable future!

Weaver and Haymaker are adamant on critical need for soil mineralization in regard to health, stating that food without mineralization has greatly reduced nutritional value, and mineralized food supports supreme well-being and longevity.

> Virtually all subsoil and most topsoil of the world have been stripped of all but a small quantity of elements [primarily by agriculture]. So it is not surprising that the chemical-grown corn had substantially less mineral content than the 1963 corn described in the USDA Handbook of the Nutritional Contents of Food..
>
> As elements have been used up in the soil a poor food supply in 1963 turned into a 100 percent junk food supply in 1978. There has been a corresponding increase in dis-ease and medical costs. Essentially, dis-ease means that enzyme systems are malfunctioning for lack of the elements required to make the enzymes.
>
> Hunza is a small country in a high Himalayan mountain valley. Health, strength and longevity of the Hunzacuts is legendary. A key factor is irrigation of valley soils with a milky-colored stream from the meltwater of the Ultar glacier. The color comes from the mixed rock ground beneath the glacier. The people are virtually never sick. They do not develop cancer. Many are active workers at 90; some live to be 120. These facts are well documented, yet the world's "health professionals" ignore them while continuing the hopeless search for man-made "cures."
>
> *John D. Haymaker (1914-1994) & Don Weaver*
> *The Survival Of Civilization: Carbon Dioxide, Investment Money, Population –*
> *Three Problems Threatening Our Existence*

What do we think exotic Superfoods will do for us? Our hope is they will help us be less tired, have more energy, be more beautiful, sexy, vital, handsome, slimmer, fit, beautiful skin thicker hair Right? ...the external "fix." Even if they give us such results, the reason is because they are providing high frequency mineralized nourishment to our cells inducing electromagnetics that support flow of Life-force. Exotic Superfoods are wonderful, delicious, fun and excellent for the Body. They give us the boost to live more vital Lives, because they have evolved harmoniously with our Earth Mother.

Our commercial food supply is literally "foodless," profoundly lacking mineralization that Creates Life-force. In this case, ignorance is not bliss; if we keep running like lemmings toward this cliff, humanity may have to start over again. This is a less than happy future for for our children, grandchildren, great grandchildren, their children's children, and a sad ending for a very bright civilization. A critical move toward a viable future requires stepping out of this old "dying" system, growing a home garden in highly mineralized soil, and/or participating in the global movement to remineralize soils for our future survival as a species. Find a way to contribute or volunteer at Remineralize dot org

Does the average person realize, when eating a "cheap" hamburger at McDonald's, deforestation of rainforest to grow the beef they're eating is driving us toward another Ice

Age and potential extinction? Ignorance is not bliss. We are living unsustainably and must change to move toward a viable future, how cool that we are educated enough to understand this. A small movement of the rudder will land us at a different place on the shore. Our individual choices are critical to where we land as a civilization of the future.

Although you may have lived most of your Life this way, we encourage you to wake up out of the mindset that there must be an instant cure for everything. Marketing and our societal mindset would like us to think so; this is exactly how billions are made off pain and suffering. Foundational Living in harmony with Nature and Mother Earth are critical to our very survival itself. Perhaps it might be worthwhile to consider selling your business or moving away from your current Life, and immersing yourself and family into a viable Planetary future. Believe it or not, EVERY PERSON makes a huge difference!

The truest answer is that we Wake Up. The true solution, the true magic pill, is dedication to higher ideals and practices, and the path of the Heart, harmonizing with Earth Mother Gaia. Cultivating Lifestyle to nourish Well-Being, we gradually open the door within, to be proactive in our Life and the World. Meanwhile, consuming Superfoods can help us have the regenerative energy, ability and power to do it!

> Man cannot discover new oceans unless he has the
> courage to lose sight of the shore.
>
> *Andre Gide (1869-1951) Nobel Prize Literature, 1947*
> *Wrote on freedom and empowerment in the face of moralistic and puritanical constraints*

Walking in balance with our Earth Mother, learning to harmonize our lives with our amazing ecosystem, Living at Cause rather than Effect is the prime objective of *21st Century Superhumans*. Here are more of John Haymaker and Don Weaver's reminders about *real* secrets to good health, well-being and our very survival itself:

Ten thousand years ago the Mississippi Valley was fed and built up by runoff from the glaciers. The deep deposit of organically-enriched alluvial soil in Illinois attests to a long period of luxuriant plant growth. Yet, when the settlers plowed the valley, they did not find topsoil that would give the health record of the Hunzacuts. Ten thousand years of leaching by a 30-inch annual rainfall is the difference. Man can stay on this Earth only if the glacial periods come every 100,000 years to replenish the mineral supply—or man gets bright enough to grind the rock himself.

There are several other places in the world similar to Hunza, such as the Caucasus Mountains in Russia where 10 percent of the people are centenarians. There are glaciers in the mountains. Regardless of where it is that people attain excellent health and maximum Life, it can be traced to a continual supply of fresh-ground mixed rocks flowing to the soil where their crops are grown.

Thus the secret of good health and long Life lies not in the fountain of youth or in a chemical company's laboratory, but in the acceleration of the natural biological processes. Failure to remineralize the soil will not just cause a continued mental and physical degeneration of humanity but will quickly bring famine, death, and glaciation in that order. Glaciation is nature's way of remineralizing the soil.

Doesn't this make you want to go out and grow your own or neighborhood garden, enrich the soil with rock dust and other organic matter, envision yourself, family, friends and community with juicy gardens and orchards, healthier and more vital, supporting remineralization of the Planet? Our minds are even brighter, when we are well nourished and mineralized; and again this is the cycle of Cause and Effect as we learn to understand and harmonize our lives with the natural ecosystem in which we are designed to Live.

Odd as I am sure it will appear to some, I can think of no better form of personal involvement in the cure of the environment than that of gardening. A person who is growing a garden, if growing it organically, is improving a piece of the world. They are producing something to eat, which makes them somewhat independent of the grocery business, and they are also enlarging for themselves and others, the meaning of food and the pleasure of eating.

Wendell Berry , Author, Activist, Farmer
The Art of the Commonplace: The Agrarian Essays

Do you know what makes a Superfood a Superfood? Many of them are from plants going back thousands of years, surviving natural selection. This means the strongest and healthiest traits are carried on from generation to generation, making the food source within the plant of exceptional quality. In addition many super foods tend to have evolved in a naturalized setting within a forest or ecosystem. Again this means they have picked up minerals and natural elements that more cultivated varieties may not contain. Similar benefits exist with wild foods and foraging.

Superfood guru, David Wolfe maintains, "Superfoods are an essential part of a balanced diet and allow us to get more nutrition with less eating."

Superfoods comprise a specific set of edible nutritious plants that cannot be classified as foods or medicines, because they combine positive aspects of both.

David Wolfe
Superfoods: The Food and Medicine of the Future

Drop down into the Heart with Deep Gratitude, aligning frequency, when taking in Raw Superfoods. These High Vibrational foods become alchemically One with the body and raise our Frequency. As we Lighten up our Being with Superfoods, with Gratitude to Pachamama, the Earth Mother, we make a difference by Living inspired energized lives as *21st Century Superhumans*!

Following is a partial list of exotic Superfoods now popularly available, delicious added to smoothies and green shakes, eaten alone or added to raw Creations.

GOGI BERRY is a sweet red fruit native to Asia, and has been used as a medicinal food for thousands of years. It is s a noted food of many centurians living active lives to well-over 100. With high protein, 21 essential minerals, and 18 amino acids, the goji berry is a nutrient-dense superfood in a class all its own; once you get started on it, you'll be hooked.

CACAO obtained raw, dried at low temperature, is a completely different food then the processed chocolate with which we are familiar. The crunchy "nibs" can be chewed whole, or added ground to shakes and sweet treats. Cacao is super-high in antioxidants, contains magnesium, sulfur, benefits cardio, skin, hair and immune systems. Cacao increases endorphins and has been used ceremonially for thousands of years in South America to open the Heart. Native to central and South America, the cacao is delightful when picked fresh, commonly made into a beverage including it's natural cocoa butter, without theobromine of the seeds.

HEMPSEED comes from the Cannabis plant, a different variety than the "herb." Hempseed is an amazing food, containing all essential amino acids and fatty acids necessary to maintain Life, with close to complete amino acid profile. 30-35% weight of hempseed is hemp oil, 80% essential fatty acids (EFAs) more balanced than flax, (which can Create a deficiency in GLA). Hemp farming is a great way to go. It is fast growing, renewable, sustainable, and can replace much of what we use trees (producing fiber for cloth and rope, building materials, paper, and high quality oil, protein and herb).

MACA was revered by the Incas for endurance and to increase stamina; they also used it to recover from illness as it is an adaptogen. According to folk belief, it has a legendary ability to deliver energy, mental clarity and enhance sex drive. It contains sterols (can have similar effects), should be used in small quantities and off and on rather than daily.

SALT - unpolluted salts from the sea and ancient sea beds contain full mineral complexes that are preferable to commercial salt. Real Salt and Sea Salt particularly Celtic are some of the best. Himalayan contains many minerals too. Variety is good to access various mineral complexes. Westin Price found that when people in primitive cultures accessed greens, they did not travel as much for salt. This is good advice to us. A high frequency salt in small amounts can add mineralization to our food, and optimum is developing highly mineralized soil and eating fresh greens grown in it.

OTHER SUPERFOODS include numerous exotic and delicious fruits, berries, nuts, seeds, herbs and spices. Get to know them and how they feel to your Body, gradually incorporate and enjoy the benefits of these Light filled nutrition sources.

Life-Force is the greatest "Superfood nutrient." We can measure protein, fat, carbohydrates, vitamins and minerals, yet if the food is "low frequency," it depletes Life rather than supporting it. It is important to become aware that most commercially available food has *little* Life-Force. This is one reason we have become addicted to caffeine and other stimulants, because we're missing natural vitality that comes from Live foods. Dead processed foods require enzymes to digest and assimilate, robbing them from vital bodily functions, diminishing Life force. Change your Life Now, adopt a Superfoods *Live-it!*

Dr. Edward Howell's book *Enzyme Nutrition* from 1898 is a *classic* essential reference for understanding enzymes as spark plugs of Life. Distinction between Raw and Living foods is based on enzyme content and Life Force. *Raw food* is "mature," such as apples or lettuce picked from garden or orchard when ripe. *Living food* such as sprouts and grasses, are harvested in the first seven days of Life after the seeds sprout. During this first 7 days cells rapidly multiply and enzymes are far more abundant than they will be at any other time in the Life of the plant. Sprouts and young grasses regenerate the body; wheatgrass and sprouted/Living Food programs work well to reverse degenerative conditions for vitality and regeneration. Powerful Lifestyle choices incorporate these elements.

Seeds contain enzyme inhibitors to keep them dormant until the next growing season. When we eat wheat ground to flour, it contains enzyme inhibitors designed to protect the dormant seed. Once soaked in water and sprouting beings, enzyme inhibitors are washed away, the seed becomes a Living sprout, and is much more nutritious. This is why we suggest sprouted grain or Ezekiel bread as a first choice for breads, tortillas, crackers, etc.

Fresh, Raw, Living Foods transmit Life and are ultra-easy to digest. Their enzymes contribute to cellular Life-force rather than taking from it. When nutrition is at least 50% Raw and Living Food, it is of **huge benefit**; we are leaner with more energy and youthfulness. Fresh salads, sprouts, green shakes, vegetables, fresh fruit, juices and Superfoods are a daily mainstay for greater vitality. Integrating Raw and Living foods into our *Live-it*, is essential to Well-Being, a must for **21st Century Superhumans**.

Every long-lived culture around the World has some sort of fermented or cultured food such as sauerkraut, kimchee, yogurt, kombucha, miso or tamari as part of their everyday cuisine. Always include fermented foods in your *Live-it*. They contain beneficial enzymes, probiotics and Life force that assist digestion, small and large intestine and body enzymes.

Having used regenerative foods for many years, we notice the difference in just a day or two of heavier foods when visiting or traveling. It is super-fun to eat, Live and think Lightly, bringing energy and vitality to Life of self, family and friends! Lifestyle habits are either adding to Life or taking it away. *You pick!* It may require major Lifestyle changes to implement these things, yet worth it! Be sure to check out our website and videos for tips and quick, easy support of these Lifestyle habits! ♥

Part 4: BODY
Chapter 5
Naturally Attractive Hair, Skin, Body

To LOVE beauty is to see LIGHT.

Victor Hugo (1802-1885)
Writer, Artist, Statesman
Les Miserables, Hunchback of Notre-Dame

It's exciting we are moving toward self-acceptance with natural hair, skin and Body styles. Being fit with glowing skin and hair and a bright Smile from the Heart is Always "In." We encourage moving this direction! The closer you get to "natural," the more you will LOVE it!

BODY: LOVE yours! Commit to Being naturally healthy and attractive from inside-out. Implement *21st Century Superhuman Quantum Lifestyle!*

Follow instructions in all Chapters on cleansing, detox and nutrition. Be sure to include time outdoors, and if living in a winter climate or indoors a lot, Vitamins D3 & K2. *Check out our additional books and videos on weight loss, recipes, fitness, radiance and more.* Smile.

NOTE: **Whatever we put on skin or hair appears in the organs within 56 seconds!** Healthy Lifestyle with high frequency nutrition and cleansing makes skin and hair radiant! Reduce use of products containing items you wouldn't eat. Experiment till you find what works best for you.

HAIR PURPOSE: Our hair is our antenna, receiving electromagnetic Cosmic waves and energies, emitting our neurological signals to our surroundings. Hair is an extension of the nervous system, transmitting our energy from the brain into the outer environment, so when hair is cut, receiving and sending transmissions are dampened. One story reports the US military enrolled Native American trackers who lost psychic and tracking ability when hair was cut. Sikhs and many "masters" such as Moses, Buddha, Jesus, Shiva had long hair.

HAIR CARE: The first rule for healthy hair is a *Live-it,* rich in micro-nutrients and high frequency foods. Hair can be washed-rinsed with water containing a dash of vinegar for dark hair or a dash of lemon-lime juice for light. Gently clean hair and scalp with fingertips and rinse. It is amazing how healthy and vibrant hair becomes doing this a short time, without any commercial products! Cultivate a hair style requiring minimal cuts and products that suits you and your Lifestyle. It may take a few weeks for your hair to adjust.

Commercial products rob hair of it's natural beauty. Even healthy shampoo strips hair of natural oils, "healthy" conditioners contain polymers, silicones (plastics). If using get sulphur-free shampoo & polymer free conditioner, and give hair a rest as often as possible.

Nourish hair with avocado, leave in 1/2 hour and rinse; or apply a *tiny* bit of edible oil such as olive or coconut rubbed on palms of hands smoothed lightly through hair while wet during quiet time. Rub a bit of favorite essential oils into scalp and hair, rosemary excellent (good for memory). Comb or pic gently in shower to detangle. *Take a month to test it out. See if hair feels like the magnetic extension of your Higher senses it was designed to be.*

SKIN PURPOSE: The skin is the largest eliminative organ of the body. When overloaded the skin takes over. Toxins show up as oil, acne, blemishes or dry. First rule of healthy skin is cleanse and detox internally, and high frequency living foods. Good elimination is essential for smooth, alive skin. A simple first step is to add ground golden flaxseed to your *Live-it.* Follow instructions in chapters on cleansing, detox and nutrition. Check our videos.

SKIN CARE: Natural skin brush wet or dry. Reduce or eliminate use of soap except when dirty or to clean odor. Best to put on skin a light amount of olive oil or coconut oil. If skin is oily, clean with *dilute* hydrogen peroxide, vinegar or witch hazel. If desiring products, only use most natural, with organic, wildcrafted ingredients, such as *Annmarie Gianni.*

SUNSCREEN: We are solar Beings. Vitamin D is made in our Body by exposure to the sun, and is more than a vitamin, it is a hormone precursor. Without proper amounts of solar exposure and vitamin D3, our genetic structure becomes destabilized, as D3 is involved in regulation of over 2,000 genes. Getting outdoors in the sun increases longevity and vitality. Learn how to use Vitamins D & K2 (Read: *The Miraculous Results of Extremely High Doses of Sunshine Hormone* by Jeff Boles). If sunscreen is desired, find products with edible ingredients - make your own mixture with these Oils & SPFs: Coconut 2-8, Olive 2-8, Avocado 4-15, Raspberry Seed Oil 28-50, Almond 5, Jojoba 4, Shea Butter 3-6, Macadamia 6, Carrot Seed Oil 38-40. Include vinegar with the oil to protect and balance skin's pH. Add a little carrot seed oil for natural protection 38-40. Use SPF clothing and hat to shade body.

TEETH: Brush-floss regularly. Rather than fluoridated toothpaste, use one or more: baking soda, diluted hydrogen peroxide, occasional sea salt. ***Oil pulling*** is an excellent Ayurvedic technique, to whiten and clean teeth and detoxify body. Swish 1 T sesame or coconut oil in a.m. 15-20 min. Spit out. Brush w/above. *More in our videos and at our website!* LOVE U! ♥

Part 4 Body: Section 2
How To Cleanse And Detox

My body is a projection of my consciousness.

Deepak Chopra MD
Natural Physician, New Thought Author

I t is amazing to recognize that our body reflects our consciousness; that all dis-comfort, dis-ease, illness and mental or physical pain is Vibrational expression of thought-emotion Not of LOVE. This may take a little practice to decipher, so use our tools from Part 2: MIND to assist with clarity. Quantum Lifestyle of the *21st Century Superhuman* integrates cleansing and detox habits into daily Life to clear old toxins (a product of  Mind-energy in the physical), to support restoring well-being.

A Clean Body harmonizes and brightens the Radiance of our Being, to reflect more Light, which can be observed in images of the the human aura. Get more effective physical cleanses, by also resolving root cause by clearing thought-emotion coming up from the unconscious. Physical cleansing *combined* with mental clearing offers deeper, more productive and lasting results. As Dr. John Ray used to tell us, *"Our Perfect Electronic Blueprint already exists, all we have to do* is *step into it."* Cultivating a clean system, allows us to merge easily with our perfect blueprint resonating from LOVE.

Integrate habits of cleansing, detox and nutrition. Harmonize Body for optimum Well-Being in sync with 5th Universal Law of Rhythm, as waves go in and out from the shore:

• Sleep at night provides opportunity for digestive system to rest. Sleep on empty stomach, allow organs to rest in nightly "mini-fast."

• Upon arising *flush* what the body eliminated at a cellular level during the night. Have 1 qt. warm water plain, with lemon or pinch baking soda (to alkalize).

• Daylight Body energy supports digestion, assimilation, burning of energy; earlier is better for taking in nutrition, 3-5 hrs before bed, so Body can cleanse at night.

• Longer fasts or cleanses harmonize with yearly cycles such as spring/fall.

Incorporate cleansing and detox into your daily routine to *feel Lighter*. Most healthy nourishment is also cleansing. Remember the 6th Universal Law *Cause and Effect:*

Chance is but a name for Law not recognized; there are many planes of causation, but nothing escapes the Law. Every thought-emotion, word and action sets in motion an effect that materializes.

J.H. Tilden M.D. wrote *Toxemia Explained: The True Interpretation of The Cause of All Dis-Ease* in the 1800s. His key principle true then and now was that the body must run as a "clean machine." Our cells, bloodstream, organs and glands, take in nourishment and eliminate waste. When any of these systems are overloaded, acute conditions result such as exhaustion, cold, flu or fever Body's supreme efforts to detox.

Even epidemics are representative of a toxic cultural condition from predominant habits such as excessive meat consumption and refined foods, with perhaps cultural thought patterns thrown in. Pharmaceutical companies may take advantage of this offering the "next great vaccine," when better results would be obtained by teaching the culture to cleanse, detox and use high frequency nutrition.

Excess toxicity and repeated acute conditions continued over years, result in "organic damage" known as chronic degenerative conditions such as cancer, heart dis-ease, arthritis and others. Tilden's statement in review:

So-called dis-ease was a toxemic crisis, and when toxins were eliminated below the toleration point, the sickness passed - automatically health returned. But the dis-ease was not cured; for if cause is continued, toxins still accumulate, and in due time another crisis appears. Unless the cause is discovered and removed, crises will recur until functional derangements give way to organic dis-ease.

J.H. Tilden MD (1851-1940)
Toxemia Explained: The True Interpretation of The Cause of All Dis-Ease

There is one way, and one way alone to get and keep the Body well. Once you know this secret, you will be able to *stay* well, *avoid* illness being "passed around," escape and evade degenerative conditions *and* enter a state of youthful regeneration! As Tilden says, "The true interpretation of the cause of dis-ease and how to cure is an obvious sequence, the antidote to fear, frenzy and the popular mad chasing after so-called cures." It requires dedication, self-education and discipline in Lifestyle patterns to establish long lasting Vitality and Well-Being, that sustain us throughout Life in extraordinary ways.

This venerable secret is *"keep your "house" clean!"* Unless our Body is clean and well-nourished it cannot do the job it is designed to do. All its energy goes into efforts to cleanse and restore balance. Every illness is simply the body's attempt to "clean house" of old residue. Today's buzzwords for toxemia are *inflammation* and *acidity*. We are about to learn how to use a super cleansing system to clean the "house we live in" for lasting regenerative effects, with tricks easy to implement in busy Lives. ♥

Part 4: BODY
Chapter 6
"7 Days" To A new YOU!

Whether we acknowledge it or not, we all have a choice to be either accomplices in the status quo or everyday revolutionaries. We have a choice whether to succumb to the cultural trance, eat fast food, and race by each other in the night, or to build lives of caring, substance, and healing. So much depends on that choice.

John Robbins
Founder EarthSave, Diet for a new America

Our most productive energy flows through the creative *Essence* of our True Being LOVE, embodied best in a detoxified Body and Mind. Physical and mental cleansing brings clarity to Body-Mind, more easily transmitting Heart Coherence, Smile, Breathing, and High-Frequency thought-emotional patterns of LOVE.

HOW TO CHANGE A HABIT! EASY PEASY: Research shows that in just a few days we develop *new neurological pathways, becoming very strong by day 7*. Within 4 weeks or 28 days *entirely new habits* have formed *Neurologically*. Old less-used pathways atrophy, and a New bump forms so the distance the tiny "electric shock" jumps to send the new message is shorter than the old. *So the new habit literally encodes into our physiology.* Yes there is

great potential even for those with long ingrained habits to make real changes in lifetime pattern. It is just a matter of staying in the new routine long enough for neurology to shift.

Our brain and nervous system continually update perceptions about our current "reality," interpreting it for survival. There is no need to be "stuck in the past" (including yesterday or five minutes ago), as New neurological pathways for processing our "reality" are continuously developing. With every override of old responses and habit patterns, we Create New neural pathways, thus our clearing and goal canceling is also important.

There is no mental event that does not have a neural correlate.

Deepak Chopra MD
Natural Physician, New Thought Author

Repetition develops larger neurons and new branches or synapses like twigs on a tree. As old neurological pathways are less used, they shrink and disappear with non-use. When we change our kitchen set-up and food availability, cultivate a new social circle or put ourselves into a fresh environment such as a live-in education program, we offer ourselves the best opportunity to fire New signals in our neurobiology, and *consistently* embed the New "code." Such change of environment is a Mind-choice that integrates physiologically.

There is a difference between knowing
the path and walking the path.

Morpheus, The Matrix

Every experience is for our learning and should not be judged as success or failure, it is simply helping us discover how to steer our course. Be loving, patient and kind both with others and self, while integrating these concepts into Life. Cultivate the image that we each already exist in our "Perfect Blueprint", and we are simply on a journey of discovering alignment with it. There is no such thing as a mistake! It is all just learning along the way.

If you can dream—and not make dreams your master
If you can think—and not make thoughts your aim
If you can meet with Triumph and Disaster
And treat those two impostors just the same

Rudyard Kipling (1835-1936)
First and Youngest recipient of Nobel Prize Literature 1907

Taking good care of ourselves, then *going back* to old habits gives us contrast to make better choices next time. We may bounce around like this at first, but stay with it. Staying "neutral," Loving ourselves and the Truth of our experience, being at peace with the choices we make ultimately empower us to a new path, as we go through the learning curve of changing our patterns. Freeing ourselves from old paradigm ways of thinking, it is LOVE, not punishment or judgment that instills a New path. Positive reinforcement works best with pets, and us too!

It's important to learn to not give up when we "fall or fail" – to learn from our experience, LOVE ourselves, pick up and go on. It requires much more than just a passing interest to find vitality and well-being. It requires commitment of Lifestyle and habit. These traits begin with dedication and commitment to choosing what we've discovered is best for us. We will do more out of LOVE than anything else. LOVING Self, LOVING our process, LOVING our New choices; Breathing, Smiling.

What we "do" day-in and day-out is cumulative and adds up over time, so the highest % of our regular habits becomes our central theme. We like the 80/20 rule: if we do what's "best" 80% of the time, the other 20% takes care of itself. Repetition develops New neuro-receptors, integrating patterns in brain and nervous system. The more often we make a desired choice the more easily it happens the next time. As we participate in our own journey of cultivating healthy habits, it eventually emerges as our own personalized, miraculous way of Living, reflecting our radiance and well-being in the World. Remember, laugh, play and have fun with it!

Loving and accepting ourselves just as we are, is the most important habit to cultivate, for it helps us flow from what's truly inside us rather than responding to external pressure. By accepting, trusting, allowing and Loving ourselves and our process as it occurs, we eventually come to the point where new habits result from authentic desire flowing from within because we LOVE it! Loving Ourselves, Honoring Ourselves and every choice is the Quickest Way to Success...

> It's of no use walking anywhere to preach
> unless our walking is our preaching.

> *St. Francis of Assisi (1182-1226)*
> *Order of St. Francis*

Most of us, even those somewhat Awake, have spent much of our lives overcoming deficits we have blamed on parents, circumstances or genes. At this point we are learning they were not at fault, perhaps acting out their own deep pain, suffering and "Power Person Dynamic." *AND we drew them in and they us,* because of "matching resonance or Vibration for us to Mirror to one another what needed to be cleared from the unconscious and restored to LOVE.

Historian and Author of *Fingerprints of the Gods,* Graham Hancock, calls us a civilization with cultural *amnesia,* as we are missing critical records from advanced civilizations in antiquity who left us important clues. Within our DNA is the gene potential to operate as highly intelligent, creative Beings of LOVE and Light. *We are now learning* how to switch on our dormant 97% "junk" DNA. If we suddenly become curious as to why we have only 3% operational DNA, when a tree frog has 17% active DNA, answers lie in pre-historical accounts, Now becoming available thanks to modern technology.

Michael Tellinger's research and documented theories in *Adam's Calendar* and *Slave Species of the Gods* suggest a strong probability that we, like *Sleeping Beauty,* fell into a deep sleep long ago, with some of our DNA *turned off* so we would perform as an "obedient and hard working race." We are just now waking up to our true potential as Creator Beings, which we are stepping into very likely for the first time in history of humankind. We might imagine our DNA like Legos, lying in a pile, waiting for us to pick them up and put them back together.

The only currently known method for turning on our dormant DNA, was established by HeartMath®'s progressive research, showing that in Heart Coherence: LOVE,

Compassion, Gratitude, non-judgement, Unity, Oneness, we restructure and activate more DNA codons. We are called forth as *21st Century Superhumans* to embrace this state of being, based 100% in our True Design LOVE. This is *the resonance* that increases our well-being and vitality, and activates our 97% "sleeping" DNA. *Wow! Get ready because here we come!*

Turning on our 97% dormant DNA:

• *We activate our DNA by integrating Heart Coherence as our "normal state,"* and being fully present in Heart Coherence at all times. This is True Science of Higher Living, where LOVE, Compassion and Gratitude are the most powerful 3 words or states of BEING we ever embrace!!! Make them part of every Now Moment. This means integrating new perceptions when we see horrible things still going on in the World (rather than hatred). This is what Yeshua-Jesus meant about "turning the other cheek." As we shift our resonance to LOVE and inspire others to do the same all residual of darkness will fade. As we enter the future together in Pure LOVE, we will not even have memory of these things, because they will be erased from all timelines as LOVE was held for them. Breathe. Smile.

• Prime objective for *EVERY* **21st Century Superhuman:** *Restore our True Design, LOVE.* This is the path to Genius, Creativity, Productivity, and *the most powerful tool to change the Structure of our "Reality."* Change yourself. Change the Whole. **Arc the Hologram NOW!!!**

• *Cleansing the Body* assists us to hold High Vibrational Frequencies of LOVE, Light and Heart Coherence. Our Body is the Vehicle for our neurobiology, our biocomputer, our Mind-Energy, and Coherent Heart torus-field to resonate into the World with *our Greatest Creative Potential.*

• Releasing, *letting go old thought-emotional energy* carried in the unconscious (lower part of the iceberg) and conscious (tip of the iceberg), removes Vibrations Not of LOVE, so our *Attention in the Field manifests through our True Design LOVE. Yeshua-Jesus came to Earth to get us going this direction, with the Ancient Aramaic Forgiveness process.* If it had been understood in the culture of the day, we would be Living in a different World Now. Critical key to accessing our higher potential is *clearing our unconscious* of any and all resonance Not of LOVE with *Ancient Aramaic Forgiveness Freedom Tools* and Goal Canceling process [Part 2: MIND].

One man tells his amazing story of being infected with one of the most virulent forms of HIV as a hospital medical lab tech. He took the recommended medications, became extremely emaciated, and did not feel there was any reason to go on living. He was led to an *ayahuasca* shamanistic ceremony at a church in the Netherlands, which activated his DMT, taking him on an amazing inward "journey." He saw his DNA as curled and disconnected segments; in his "journey" he was directed to straighten out and reconnect it, which he did. From that day forward he began to get well, and lives to tell about it nine years later. We are *so much more* that just physical devices, it is critical that we grasp this, Activating Body-Mind-Heart with LOVE.

We are getting to the core, the bottom root level of why we express dis-ease and dis-comfort in Mind-Body. We are *Breaking Free* from a thought-emotional imprisonment, robbing us of our birthright of regenerative vitality and long Life. It is suggested by Michael Tellinger that in our non-functioning DNA, we have potential for continual physical regeneration and either much longer Lives or some sort of physical immortality.

As we release Not of LOVE thought-emotion our human bio-computer is *upgrading its program*. This natural Evolutionary process merges with a New holographic "reality," tuning us to Higher frequencies of Light and LOVE. Flowing aspects of self activate this shift. Examples are demonstrated in new children born with more codons already turned on in their DNA, resulting in 30% higher intelligence, telepathic skills and greater self-actualization at a young age. Even adults shifting to non-judgement, Unity and LOVE are having *their* DNA restructure.

> Then they found another kid with these codons turned on...then 10,000, then 100,000, then a million...UCLA, by watching world-wide DNA testing, estimates that 1% of the world has this new DNA. That breaks down to approximately 60 million people who are not human by the old criteria.
>
> *Drunvalo Melchizedek*
> *Ancient Secret of the Flower of Life Vol. 1*

Parents, grandparents and extended family have the opportunity to nurture this Higher intelligence and advanced DNA. It activates us to "wake up," as we adapt to and Create a hospitable environment for these young carriers of more advanced and awakened DNA to grow and develop. They will inherit the path that carried humanity into the future. The more we adjust our lives to support this evolving consciousness, the greater gifts there will be for us and those who come after.

Since the 1980s a new wave of humans have been arriving on Earth, with more codons turned on in their DNA (24 as opposed to the usual 20). UCLA's studies have found over a million with this advanced DNA, children all over the World who have paranormal abilities, including resistance to all disease including HIV/AIDS and Cancer. Drunvalo Melchizedek reports in an interview, that this seems to be spreading like a wave through our culture, with the expanded DNA even activating in adults.

> It is a very specific emotional, mental body response – a waveform coming off the body that is causing the DNA to mutate in a certain way. I've sat with Gregg Braden who was one of the first persons to write about this and what we believe is that there are 3 parts to this phenomenon. The first part is the mind that sees Unity. It sees the Flower of Life. It sees everything interconnected in all ways. It doesn't see anything as separate.
>
> And the second part is being centered in the heart – to be Loving.

And the third thing is to step out of polarity – to no longer judge the world. As long as we are judging the world as good or bad, then we are inside polarity and remain in the fallen state. I believe these people (with the new DNA) have somehow stepped out of judging and are in a state where they see everything as one and feeling LOVE.

Whatever they are doing within themselves is producing a waveform that when seen on computer screens looks almost identical to the DNA molecule. So the researchers think that by the very expression of their Life that these people are mapping with the DNA – resonating it – and are changing these 4 codons and in so doing become immune to the dis-ease.

Interview by Diane with Drunvalo Melchizedek

By Enoch Tan, new Earth Daily #1 Source for Positive News

We have this amazing piece of research done by HeartMath Institute, that when a person is in Heart Coherence, based in LOVE-Compassion-Gratitude, they literally straighten out curves in their own DNA and that of others! This essentially leads us to the conclusion that we have the amazing capacity to reactivate nonfunctioning portions of our 97% "junk" DNA *when in Heart Coherence*. During this research they found that a person *not* in Heart Coherence could *not* straighten out the DNA.

Grasping and understanding this single idea is a critically powerful tool for changing ourselves, our World and all of humanity, Now and into past and future of the 'No - Time' Continuum to shift all timelines. We have just barely tapped into our potential in this area. We activate more of our DNA potential as we integrate Heart Coherence more deeply and it becomes our natural, consistent mode of operation. *Integrating Heart Coherence is a primary practice* of **21st Century Superhumans**, similar to martial arts, meditation, chanting and prayer used by "Great Masters" of the ages.

During these Cosmic Activations, we are being inspired to Lighten up the physical Body-Mind also. As we clear old thought-emotional patterns to LOVE, and Lighten up physical habits, we increase our capacity to Live Joyful, Fulfilling Masterful Lives. Shedding physical toxicity, we also shed toxic Mind-Energy as we give Attention to our focus, Breathing, Smiling and canceling goals [Part 2: MIND].

We encourage you to enter this powerful planetary Ascension wave, by adopting **Quantum Lifestyle** habits to upgrade YOU energetically. YOU will be able to let go of shadows of victim mentality, and gain the resilience to Master YOUR existence. At this point YOU will be fully able to shape YOUR "reality" by choice.

In this fast paced world it is too frequently the case that people accept what society, family members and the authorities, whom nobody ever seems to question, believe regarding how to live their lives. And yet, the happiest people I know have been those who have accepted the primary responsibility for their own spiritual and physical well-being - those who have inner strength, courage, determination, common sense and faith in the process of creating more balanced and satisfying lives for themselves.

Dr. Ann Wigmore (1909-1993)
"Grandmother" Founder of Wheatgrass and Living Foods programs

Along with restructuring physical habits we integrate our Quantum knowing and change history, simply by upgrading our Mind-Energy about ourselves in our Newly formed "reality." This means if we've thought of ourselves as being a particular way (*i.e.* weight, smoking, dis-ease, drugs, poverty) for a long "time," we will get over it, shift the Hologram, transform our history and "Create" a New state of Being.

When you identify and hold your thought purely, on any topic for 17 seconds, it is enough to set the Universe into motion, and the Universe which has Infinite ability and resources to match the Vibration of your being, will do so.

Esther Hicks
The Teachings of Abraham, 17 Seconds

Once we incorporate our new patterns we become an example to others - not so much by what we speak - by our Vibrational presence that surrounds how we Live. Respect each person's journey, allowing his/her perfect process of choice and discovery. We cannot know the path of another unless we "walk in their shoes;" so making our own choices without control or judgment, allowing others their growth process, releases us from worrying about what someone else does or does not do. Even if it seems like the "ship" of someone close to us "may be sinking," we still allow them their perfect journey of unfolding, reminding them that we LOVE and care, while honoring their choices! Breathe. Smile. Laugh. Release and let go, and ALL will change.

Years ago, when I was first changing my Lifestyle around age 18-20, making different choices than most, my rambunctious friend, J.B., harassed me continually about what I was doing. Ten years later, I ran into him after a long absence and he said, "I know I gave you a hard time back then because I wanted to see what you were made of. You Living what you believed completely changed my Life. I now live and teach similarly to you." Wow! What a great lesson on how we may not know the effect we have on others! Recently I saw my brother after months apart, and he had switched from coffee in the a.m. to Greenshakes. I was amazed at the wonderful rosy color on his face and how great he looked! Live Your Joy and Keep Sharing! ♥ *Cary*

We may never know how we affect another, yet we can trust that our influence goes out into the *Field* surrounding us and by virtue of our Vibration, our resonance is experienced by those around us. No one likes to be criticized or told what they *ought* to be doing. When we live our truth and follow our path Joyfully, we can count on the fact, that deep inside most peoples' Hearts are hungry for authenticity, vitality and well-being, and somewhere along the way a bit is likely to rub off. As the old saying goes, *most would rather see a sermon than hear one...Just Live your best and Be Happy!*

The lives of those who "walk their talk" have great impact in this World. Often not saying a thing, just BEING what we KNOW is the best "teaching" we can generate. After all, everything in Life is based on Vibration and frequency. Our Life resonates through the Field, entraining others to it, and magnetizing that which is like itself.

> Life is actually a circle, for a vibrant body begets well mind and emotions, and healthy mind and emotions contribute to a vibrant body.
>
> *Folk Saying*

It is a discipline, a practice and an art of the highest order, to naturally cultivate our daily Life and habits around well-being of Mind and Body; this is a Sacred Journey embracing Contentment, Vitality, Youthfulness, Peace, Longevity, Resilience and the ability to Contribute our best to Life and the Future of Humanity. With each Breath and Choice we make, we hold our Attention on the *Field of Possibilities*, and resonate our Creative presence into the World. *Let's get going on this Adventure!*

7 Days To A new YOU!

(1) KNOW YOU Create YOUR "REALITY" ♥ your Vibrational Presence and Attention on the *Field of Possibilities* calls your "reality" into form. Know you are establishing new neurological pathways and diminishing the old.

(2) PRINT 50 COPIES *ARAMAIC FORGIVENESS Freedom Tool* [Part 2: MIND]

(3) DO 1-5 WORKSHEETS NOW (from #2) on the issue(s) you would like to shift your Vibration in regard to during the next 7 days, and then the following 3 weeks. *Do your best.* Listen to Mindshifter radio for guidance *whyagain.org*

(4) 2-5 WORKSHEETS DAILY (from #2) *each day for the next 7 days!* Do them as quickly as possible, without laboring too much over whether "right or wrong." They will gradually get easier. Keep track of how many you do. Throw them away. You are done with this energy.

(5) MEAL PLAN Chapter 49, *Ideal Nutrition*, look at *LIVE-IT NUTRITION* list. Jot down your meal plan for the week, Breakfast, Lunch, Dinner, snacks, based on high frequency whole foods. Commit to following your meal plan. Whether you make your own food or eat out, Create a meal plan, based around your favorite whole natural foods.

(6) DRINK UPON ARISING DAILY warm 1/2-1 quart warm water, water with a pinch of baking soda and a wedge of lemon to alkalize and cleanse; can also add a pinch of cayenne if desired for deeper cleansing. AFTER water; tea if desired. Eliminate coffee if possible; otherwise have decaf.

(7) CANCEL GOALS each evening when you go to bed; lie flat, use gentle circular mouth Breath to keep energy open and flowing. Relax jaw. invite *Rookha d'Koodsha* (Aramaic), elemental aspect of our Being, the super-processor, to help cancel your goals. Mentally cancel goals for all thoughts causing stress, or that you're thinking about doing or accomplishing. Say to yourself, "I now cancel all my goals, conscious, subconscious, unconscious and incomplete." Choose 1 thing to accomplish in the next 24 hours and set that as your goal for the following day. You may also do this exercise in the a.m. before arising.

(8) RESET PROCESS - do this process as you start your week, and every time you feel you need a "reset" of integration with your purpose for the week. Sit, close eyes, Breathe gently, relax. You may meditate, pray, listen to music - get yourself our of "monkey mind" and into **Heart -Compassion without Judgment.** Marry Mind and Heart. Envision and experience within your week the way you would like it to unfold, all happening beautifully. Experience it as "it already IS so." Focus 17 seconds. Give it to the *Field.* Breathe. Smile.

(9) Do several quick rounds of *EFT tapping* (find our videos or FastEFT)

(10) REPEAT Reset Process again. If you feel you stumble at any time.

(11) HEART COHERENCE Focus in LOVE, COMPASSION, GRATITUDE

(12) LOVE YOURSELF. SMILE, Breathe. Flow, express your joy, creativity, and your True Design, LOVE.

(13) HONOR YOURSELF that you are building and establishing new neural pathways, that with use, become better established than the old.

The world is a mirror,
forever reflecting what you see inside yourself.

Neville Goddard (1905-1972)
Manifestation, the Promise & the Law

Suggestions - 7 Day Meal Plan

Eliminate white sugar, white flour, refined foods. Use sprouted grain bread or crackers. Reduce or eliminate meat, other animal products and most fats. Add fiber, enjoy freely fresh raw fruits and vegetables, juices, soups. Include raw fermented foods daily to boost enzymes, immune system and cleansing.

For Quick Easy Recipes get - **Super Immunity**

Secrets by Cary Ellis [app coming soon!]

(1) *Morning Flush:* 1 qt. warm water with pinch Bob's Baking Soda (non-aluminum), wedge fresh lemon or lime; or plain warm water; or plain w/lemon

(2) Tea or decaf coffee - optional

(3) *Green Shake or Smoothie* - recipe next chapter, or raw meuseli type cereal with vegan milk

(4) *Between Meals:* Allow stomach to empty. Good to have 4-5 hours between meals. Allow body to restore "fasting" equilibrium. Have only water or plain tea. (If you choose to have coffee decaf is better, as is espresso or cold pressed as they reduce acid. Coffee has a tendency to irritate liver and stomach, so can activate cravings. Reduce use if possible.)

(5) *Lunch*: Raw Juices; Salad - fresh veggies, sprouts, beans, tofu, lemon juice-olive oil, pinch earth salt, herbs. Soups - homemade, fresh veggies, quinoa, sprouted beans. Sandwich or roll-up (sprouted grain bread); veggies, tahini, almond butter.

(6) *Dinner:* Juice; Salad - fresh veggies, sprouts, beans, tofu, lemon juice-olive oil, pinch earth salt, herbs. Soup - homemade, fresh veggies, quinoa, sprouted beans. Sprouted grain bread or crackers. Rice or quinoa. Healthy international foods.

(7) *Dessert:* There are amazing, wonderful and delicious deserts available to buy at health food store or make at home using natural sweeteners.

(8) *Snacks:* Fresh fruit or veggies, juices, tea

(9) *Bedtime:* Allow 2-4 hours after dinner with stomach empty before going to bed. This gives digestive organs a well-needed rest while you sleep.

First commit. Then follow up, putting into practice New foods and habits. Enjoy!

Giving yourself just seven days to experiment with this kind of easy Cleansing Nutrition can provide such energy and Lightness of Being, that you may choose to incorporate these Quantum Lifestyle habits on an everyday basis. The **21st Century Superhuman** Journey is an exploration of our own Body-Mind, and how to optimize care and feeding for Authentic self-expression, achievement and accomplishing what we came into this World to do! ♥

Part 4: BODY

Chapter 7

Cleanse & Detox: 3 - 7 - 30 Day Cleanses

A fast, rest in bed, and the giving up of enervating habits, mental and physical will allow nature to eliminate the accumulated toxin; then if enervating habits are given up, and rational living habits adopted, health will come back to stay.

Dr. J. H. Tilden
Toxemia Explained, the True Interpretation of the Cause of Dis-Ease

Have you done a cleanse or detox? This is an opportunity to give the body a rest from dense food, increase fluids, add herbs, lighten nutrition, and use essential oils, massage or energy work to free things up and get the body flowing. It is one of the most liberating things we can do, and the feeling of "Lightness of Being" it brings is extraordinary!

Cleanses have gained popularity in recent years, as our culture is on almost continual overload, from lower frequency and excessive food, beverages and mental stress that exhaust and devitalize the system. Cleanse and detox are relatively interchangeable, and may be directed at the entire body as we are here, or organ specific *(more at our website)*. *Enervating habits* in quote above means, "To weaken or destroy the" strength or vitality of;" such as luxury or excess that destroys health.

Cleansing and detox help us recover from excesses of modern Lifestyle, and "Clean the House We Live In," to restore connection with *the sacred within*. Sun Bear was a gifted Native American medicine man and shaman, with whom Teddi, her then partner and four year old daughter were invited to spend the summer with at *Vision Mountain* retreat in Ford, Washington near Spokane 1983. Their experience with him deepened their understanding of cleansing on many levels.

We met Sun bear at a Medicine Wheel gathering in Gainesville, Florida, where we were attracted to his teaching, 'Walking in Balance on Mother Earth.' He invited us to come to Spokane, as apprentices and to assist with his vision quests. Every two weeks new apprentices arrived, and Sunday evening Sun Bear instructed them to to go up on the Mountain and cry for their vision. He told them not to come down till they knew what they had come to Earth to do, for without a mission they would walk through Life empty. "What did you come here to do? It's inside of you..."

Grandfather, look upon our brokenness... We know that in all Creation, only the Human Family has strayed from the Sacred Way. We are the ones who must come back together to walk in the Sacred Way. Grandfather, Sacred One, teach us LOVE, Compassion and Honor, that we may heal the Earth Mother Gaia and heal each other from separateness.

Sun Bear's Ojibwe Prayer

*People came from California, Germany, Mexico, Florida, Montana, all over the World, drawn by his workshops and books. Most well known was, **Walk in Balance on the Earth Mother**. This was a self-reliance retreat where participants learned gardening, food preservation and building root cellars. He taught a sacred way to take the Life of an animal if needed to be self-reliant. At the root of everything he taught was recognition of the sacred in connecting with the Earth Mother Gaia, and the importance of everyone finding their own path.*

As visitors arrived at the longhouse on Vision Mountain, Sun Bear walked among them, taking out compost, feeding chickens, chopping wood for sweat lodges, carrying water to the chicken coop. He walked among the people all day, and no one recognized him. Then at six o'clock, after the evening meal, Sun Bear changed into his medicine attire; black fringed shirt and hat, medicine beads, sacred objects, sacred rattle, sacred pipe. When he walked down the stairs, a whisper went through the room. He had walked among them all day and they had not noticed, as was his plan - teaching them to treat everyone as a sacred medicine person.

He told them to go out and find their places on the mountain for three days, draw an eight foot circle around themselves, not leave the circle and cry for their vision. He had them make their own sacred space on Mother Earth, dig a hole and empty their emotions, pain, suffering and their past into the Earth, then cry out to the their 'brothers and sisters the Stars,' until they were empty of that which did not belong, and reconnected with their True Spirit; so when they came down off the mountain they were a True Human Being...

In gentleness there is great strength, power can be a very quiet thing.

Sun Bear
Native American Shaman, Medicine Man

During the next few days, we set water and herbal tea outside each circle for the apprentices and heard their primal shouts on the wind, as they connected with Great Spirit. Sun Bear would say, 'You can call me Medicine Man, you can call me Shaman; what I'm here to do is instruct you in the ways of Great Spirit, to 'Walk in Balance on Our Earth Mother. We are ALL the Rainbow Nation. Nataqua Assay' ♥ *Teddi*

CLEARING WHAT DRIVES OUR HABITS: "Why do we perpetuate habits that require cleansing and detoxification? What is it that causes us to eat too much, heavy greasy foods, excessive animal products, beverages containing sugar, stimulants or alcohol, drugs and pharmaceuticals; consuming destructive unnatural substances to such an extent that 60 to 70% are dying of de-generative conditions?? *AND* offloading our dis-harmony to pets, with 60 to 70% of them dying of de-generative illness?? We are *regenerative* if we choose to be. It is our choice - *it takes clearing out our unconscious container of our "old pain-data-base" to access our regenerative potential.*

The deepest, most Innate aspect of our Being is constantly moving toward Union with our True Nature LOVE. Habits blocking Life Force are uncomfortable for good reason! They point to our generational and historical database, to clear it, run the anti-virus in our "computer system," remove the old thought-emotion inharmonious with Source, stored in our unconscious container, causing PAIN! When we are ready to "wake up" we release habits causing physical pain, Mirroring our shadows!

Understood by few throughout the ages, dis-comfort is an opportunity to remove old "corrupt data." It resonates louder and louder with our pain from the shadows of our personal and collective unconscious, till we notice and clear it. We are in a time of crisis for all systems surrounding us, our self-expression, our bodies, our ecosystem, governments, banking systems, our Planet and her creatures. Pain and discomfort Mirrored thought-emotion in personal and collective "realities" asks to be set Free.

THE SOLUTION is to clear all Not of LOVE thought-emotion from OURSELVES, buried in the unconscious, our *unaware* Vibration in our World. Finally, with Quantum physics, we understand what this is and **HOW** it works.

> ...referring to the multi-generational database stored in our carbon based memory; when it fires, takes over or is resonated with enough amplitude, it robs us of our awareness that we were Created by creator to act as the Active Presence of LOVE.
>
> *dr. michael ryce, whyagain.org*

Have you done a cleanse or detox, and done it again a few months later? Our objective is to clean "our house" or Body-Mind, and use habits that nourish and cleanse everyday. A periodic cleanse or detox can then be used to Lighten things up. Successful cleansing removes Body-Mind toxemia. Habits clogging our system at the root of dis-ease, are a result of Not of LOVE Mind-Energy, getting our Attention through pain, to restore LOVE.

When we are awake enough to remove remove the shadow-pain within us, we restore the ever-flowing state of Vibrancy and Vitality that is our natural birthright. Check the list below for what might be hidden in your historical memory banks; or perhaps find evidence recognizable in your bloodline. Any such issues can also be at the root of physical discomfort, illness, pain, imbalanced weight, even colds and flu.

- ☐ Beloved friend, relative or pet died; grief, sorrow, rage or guilt about it
- ☐ Adopted, do or do not know who your parents were
- ☐ Still blaming your parents for your issues
- ☐ Sexual abuse somewhere in the family
- ☐ Rage, fear or shame as a child
- ☐ Rage, fear or shame as an adult
- ☐ Panic attacks
- ☐ Don't like your body, hair or face
- ☐ Punished as a child
- ☐ Guilt or shame
- ☐ War or some other traumatic societal event (or someone close to you)
- ☐ Would like to fix the World
- ☐ Anesthetic during medical or dental procedure
- ☐ Near death experience NDE (we like to call near Life experience:)
- ☐ Drugs and or alcohol regular use or to unconsciousness
- ☐ Smoking
- ☐ Low frequency foods
- ☐ Terror or rage history in bloodline
- ☐ Can't stand to see someone or something suffer
- ☐ Rage or fear at all the terrible things going on around us
- ☐ Don't like job
- ☐ Don't like how government or economic system handling things
- ☐ Have aches, pains, illness, dis-ease
- ☐ Afraid won't be able to pay bills
- ☐ Work out of necessity or obligation with little joy
- ☐ In relationship, don't feel understood, cared for or appreciated
- ☐ Would like to have a relationship yet don't
- ☐ Strongly dislike some people
- ☐ Feel -felt abandoned
- ☐ Dreams hope to do "someday"
- ☐ Don't know if will ever do what really good at
- ☐ Other _____

Okay, did you check some boxes? *Right, not a fun list.* Many of us have trained ourselves to *not* dwell on such things. What's valuable is to bring them up from our unconscious, do goal canceling processes until the charge is gone, so they can discharge while we're also physically cleansing. The old resonance will dissolve from us and Planet Earth, as we "clean house," remembering *there is no 'out there' out there*, moving into LOVE.

Clearing thought-emotion Not of LOVE, *along with* physical cleansing and detox removes it from Body-Mind. *Thought-data crystalized in the physical structure, slows energy flow and accumulates toxins, so clearing the two together is imperative!* Dr. Wayne Dyer says,

> The unconscious is a machine,
> it replays the program unless you change it.

Clearing thought-emotion along with Body addresses toxemia at its root. If it's been there for years, it's not likely to go away on its own. This primary teaching Yeshua brought forth in Ancient Aramaic for "forgiveness" was to remove the thought-resonance from within ourselves. [Part 2: MIND] He knew it was crucial for humanity to progress, as is Now confirmed by Quantum physics and Attention on the *Field!* We are reversing a lifetime of thinking that our "misery" originates outside of us, discovering it comes from within.

EXAMPLES: Teddi comes from a family where at least five known generations of women have had the "LOVE of their life" die unexpectedly, in an unfortunate accident or war at a young age. As mysterious as it is to untangle, do you think there might be a genetic Mind-Energy holding resonance for this pattern to continue through these generations?

Teddi worked on her own process to clear shadow thoughts in her subconscious, so that this pattern would not have to carry forward in her bloodline energetically. Here are her thoughts on how this has been transformed within her, by doing her inner clearing.

When I met up with Dr. John Ray, and I was on the Body Electronics point holding table, my issues from these ongoing family circumstances arose. It was amazing how a flood of memories came up, around loss of a beloved and being left alone, not just from myself, also from my great-grandmother, grandmother, mother and daughter. It became very clear how this genetic heritage played a role in what occurred in my own life, both through subtle thoughts I had experienced and unconscious patterns "driving the boat," energetically.

As I went into the pain that came up and brought it to the conscious mental level for clearing while my points were held on the table, these energetic patterns brought to conscious awareness began to clear from my field. I was able to go forward from those sessions with a New level of freedom from things layered in my genetic past; I was able to end that genetic dysfunction. We know the World has upside down energy patterns. It is up to us to live consciously and enter into consciously creating. It is by doing this personal inner work, that we are able to change the World around us, beginning first with self and our family history past, present and future - and cleaning up our manifestation filters, resonating to others. ♥ *Teddi*

Here is how my (Cary's) genetic history has played into what I've been clearing: *I know where I get my fiery spirit and intelligence; and I also know where I got rage and terror; as my genetic heritage is partially Middle Eastern with European and a little Jewish thrown in. Over a couple of years of doing several thousand of dr. michael ryce's "goal canceling" worksheets, the more I discovered the roots of terror and rage within me. Because of what was surfacing, michael encouraged me to watch the movie **The Stoning of Soraya M**. It took me a long time, because I don't commonly watch things"upsetting." However when I finally did, it was one of the most powerful, life-changing experiences ever, because I did it along **with numerous Ancient Aramaic True Forgiveness·"goal canceling" worksheets**; diffusing energetic patterns from my genetic databank, hidden there for millennia. After the movie and clearing intensely related layers, I was able to step more powerfully into my own path and actually Create this book! [Details in Part 2: MIND]*

*I also discovered that stoning and executing those who don't abide by strict religious standards still "to my horror" exist today in some places; residual from an ignorant history, seeds of which were in my unconscious container. **The only way we will remove such things from our World, is to remove them from our own unconscious.** I have been in spiritual circles for years, and enjoy a gentle way of being; yet I learned when we are willing to step into the depths of our pain to remove the old thought-emotion holding resonance, we free these frequencies forever.*

Millions yet unborn will benefit from the work you do.

dr. michael ryce's comment
A Course In Miracles

Although I had read Zecharia Sitchin years ago, Michael Tellinger's "Slave Species of the Gods" has Now shed a bright Light on the same pre-history from Ancient tablets of Sumer; my Mind has been jostled to a deeper awareness of "stories" of why there is such suffering on Earth and within us. We are Now letting thousands of years of oppression and suffering go from within us. It is Mind-Energy. "There is no 'out there' out there." As we clear anything in the way projecting into our World, our connection with Source, LOVE shines through. ♥ *Cary [For complete understanding be sure to read Part 1: SHIFT OF THE AGES, Part 2: MIND, Part 3: SPIRIT].*

As we release "old data" from the unconscious that has been driving behavior, neurobiology and Body-Mind restructure. We see toxin patterns show up in the iris of the eye similarly in families (learn more about Iridology at our website). We bring true desires into Creation by removing these inhibiting frequencies and our bodies become Lighter!

Make your requests, concerns and desires in the language of fun...
the Universe will be quicker to respond to your needs.

Dr. Richard Bartlett
Matrix Energetics

ALL Not of LOVE, stored in the unconscious also "crystalizes" in the physical structure. We use open mouthed Breathing to assist with releasing this "old data," the physical "crystals" dissolve into water (tears), then vapor. Keep Breathing (beyond crying) through the layers to transmute ALL, release, let go and surrender. *Meditation* in Part 2 offers excellent daily clearing processes. Breathe. Smile.

Suffering comes from holding on to what does not serve our personal evolution. We let it go to make room for the new Life emerging within us. As we prepare for a cleanse or detox we "let go" on many levels. Once we clear ourselves and enter Heart Coherence with Pure LOVE, Compassion and Gratitude, we no longer accumulate "layers," and clear ourselves to Live in Pure LOVE!

> The only devil you need to be concerned about
> is the one running around in your own heart.
>
> *Mahatma Gandhi (1969-1948)*
> *Non-Violent Leader of India*

Note areas you would like to clear during your cleanse or detox. Our teachers and mentors guiding *us* on the path, taught us that once we learn to cleanse and detox, it becomes an integral part of our daily Lives. Occasionally a more in-depth retreat deepens our experience in clearing, using these experiences to go inward and achieve deeper clarity. Check our website for retreats and gatherings; also those by dr. michael ryce. We invite you to incorporate these foundational practices into your everyday Life. Live from your Heart. Live Authentically expressing True *Essence,* beyond old layers or external expectation. Breathe. Smile.

> Even a Vessel of Gold needs polishing occasionally.
>
> *Jack White (1934-1998)*
> *God's Game of Life*

CLEANSING OUR VESSEL -
DAILY PRACTICES - MIND & HEART

1. **First thing in morning connect with the Circle of Life.** Express gratitude; Breathe and Smile your prayers or meditation forward into your day. Walk outside to commune with and receive gifts of nature in your surroundings, gardens, plants, flowers, trees, water, Sun, Earth, Sky. It already knows you are coming. Feel your Oneness with everything, during your walk and putting out your prayers.

    a. Teddi says, *"First thing in the morning as the sun was coming up, Sun Bear would get me from the kitchen to take a walk and get our daily vegetables. As we walked to the garden path he would already start talking to the vegetables in the garden and say they knew we were coming. I believe he shared this with me so I would learn to feel Oneness with everything; with the onions, carrots, sorrel, anything we needed for our sustenance that day, we were already One with it. That's the kind of thought he gave his day. He knew how his whole day would unfold by doing this process."*

    b. We pray from the moment we wake up. Pray it forward. Unfold your day with prayer, thought, vision, intention. This is mastery. In our consciousness we're sitting in the Himalayas or Andes, walking the Earth plane, blessing every moment.

> Ask and it will be given to you, search and you will find, knock and the door will be opened for you. For everyone who asks, receives, and everyone who searches finds, and for everyone who knocks the door will be opened.
>
> *Matthew 7:7-8*

2. ***Clearing ripples and bubbles.*** Notice energy that is stuck, repetitive or not moving easily. Breathe into it with open mouth, smile, release and let it go. Prayers, giving it to the *Field* help clear. EFT tapping is useful here. If you are consistent with these practices, one day you will wake up and you will have shifted to a New neurobiology. Here is an example of using Light for clearing.

> Honor your Inner feelings - ...feel in every moment the energies that overlay them. Keep your Heart in a rhythm that welcomes those feelings, and deepen them with total Compassion. Compassion is the knowing impetus and the platform for connecting with all interdimensional realms.
>
> Unconditional Loving Compassion heals and reactivates the natural *Essence* of all original cellular lifeforms. Use the Violet Flame to transmute all incongruent feelings and follow with waves of Gold and White Light flowing over and purifying all in the Earth Plane. Thank you Divine Spirit.
>
> *Sharon Hall*
> *Meditative Thoughts*

3. ***"Go into the pain."*** [Dr. John Ray] Whatever comes up Not of LOVE go into it, allow it to surface until dissolves. Notice if you are feeling something about what "someone else did or is doing," remove blame, clear your thought. Cancel goals that have not been met. *"I now invite Aramaic - Rookha d'koodsha (my Divine super-processor) to help me cancel all my goals, conscious, unconscious, subconscious and incomplete."* [Part 2: MIND] With this we clear away mind-clutter that takes away from Higher focus or is based on shadow content. Notice your belief system adjusting to knowing you Create your "reality." Breathe. Smile. Welcome response from the *Field of Possibilities,* beyond your imagining. Early in this process there may be catharsis, as when Sun Bear sent apprentices to the mountain to cry for their vision, releasing all falsely programmed belief systems. We are releasing generational constructs and false expectations we believed were real.

4. ***Seek your own vision. Seek your deeper mission. Seek your True Self, your Authenticity.*** Your expression in this World will always feel lacking until you do this. Give up all falsehoods perpetuated in you to get along with partner, friends, society, family. Every

part of our Journey has value, even when we're not living our Truth, its one of the ways we get to find out what we *desire* that is our Truth and how to Live it.

"My" Perfect LOVE for you is your perfect freedom.

Jack White (1934-1998)
God's Game of Life

5. ***Fast and pray. Cleanse and detox.*** *'Follow the yellow brick road.'* Adopt Lifestyle habits that include these things *Everyday.* Do them out of LOVE. Life is a journey. *Remember, journey of a thousand miles begins with the first step...*

    a. Take note of your words and how are you are expressing your creative thought through your words. Use only positive creative words both audibly and in thought. Remember, *Yoda said, "There is no try, it is do or do not."*

6. To integrate into your being, speak it out loud or share with someone. ***Where two or more are gathered...*** Write down or share with a friend what you learned about your mission and what Great Spirit has shared with you. Always heed your inner voice.

    a. Breathe into and imagine your Life flowing with your own purpose, your own "river." Experience it "IS" in the "Now," expressing your best talents, doing things you LOVE. "I Am Now _____..."

        ii. From a Quantum perspective Dr. Richard Bartlett of Matrix Energetics emphasizes that left brain holds particles in form, and right brain entertains Quantum potential that can shift things in an instant. *Trust whatever shows up in your awareness, even if it doesn't make any sense or appear to be useful in the moment. You have a potentially infinite set of possibilities within the morphic grid of what can manifest in the very next moment. The Field is continually moving into New Creation!*

By cultivating the habit of asking powerful mind altering questions, you are training your right brain to respond to the signals from your unconscious.

Dr. Richard Bartlett
Matrix Energetics

CLEANSING OUR VESSEL - DAILY PRACTICES - BODY

INTEGRATING CLEANSING into our daily routine is a **21st Century Superhuman Quantum Lifestyle** tool for excellence! Set up daily rituals similar to brushing teeth, for example:

- Begin each day with 1 quart warm water (lemon, cayenne, opt.)
- Begin each day with lighting a candle, doing a short meditation-clearing
- Green Shake for breakfast or blended raw soup
- 2 more meals - 5 hrs. apart / vegetable based

BATHING: If you live in an area where chlorine or fluoride is added to the water, get a filter for your shower. Take a shower or bath daily. Use as few man-made shampoos, soaps, conditioners as possible. Experiment with a little vinegar in water for hair. Discover favorite essential oils for during or after bathing. Put in hair or dilute with carrier oil and use on skin. Use a skin brush to freshen and clean skin, stimulating healthy circulation. Final rinse with cool water if comfortable, to close pores and stimulate blood. Epsom Salts, Baking Soda or Magnesium Chloride can be used in soaks for good benefit.

Cleansing is part of daily routine in *Quantum Lifestyle*. Basic practices integrated over many years build a foundation for sustainable good health. A clean body, mind, spirit lays foundation for Well-Being and Vitality.

Toxemia at a cellular level lays foundation for illness. Much of our modern Lifestyle contributes to overloading the body, from overeating, excessive fats, sugars, and proteins, lack of exercise, pesticides, polluted water, chlorinated and fluoridated water, environmental toxins, vaccinations, pharmaceuticals, silver-mercury dental fillings, food additives, GMOs, negative thought and emotion, stress. So whatever we do on a regular basis to "keep our house clean" is very worthwhile.

> One of my goals each day is to fully embody the "new Way of Life" and teach by example the higher spiritual principles, which will transform this world into Light. I am constantly checking every area of my Life, in an effort to fine-tune and upgrade all my methods and perceptions.
>
> *Bryan de Flores*
> *Lightquest International*

Detoxing and cleansing have become so popular they're mainstream, even promoted by Dr. Oz, with millions of cleanses offered online, and instructions anyone can follow. Going to a natural healing center to learn how to detox or cleanse, is a great way to experience the basics, yet it can also be learned at home. Don't make cleansing "just another way to purge" or "self-punishment for overdoing." Modern civilization is built on a house of cards with constant running after illusory satisfaction to "look or feel better."

A healthy routine we can live with on a daily basis is easier than extremes for Body-Mind to restore Energy and Vitality. Set up your home as a wonderful nucleus, where Healthy Foods you Love, and routine aimed at Vitality and Inner Peace support your Journey. *21st Century Superhuman* Cleanse and Detox is about shedding false layers, finding and expressing our True Spirit and discovering our own Authentic Expression. Recovering True sense of purpose takes courage and perhaps "going against" the cultural flow. However once we reclaim this Birthright, Vitality returns!

> Take therefore no thought for the morrow:
> for the morrow shall take thought for the things of itself.
>
> *Matthew 6:34*

Play with what's here and cultivate your own routine; do what works with your Lifestyle, your personal tastes and what you discover raises *your* Vitality. Remember, once vitality increases from physical-thought-emotional cleansing, New layers are likely to surface to clear! [Part 3: SPIRIT]

It's important for each individual to seek their own path, listen to their Body and learn what is most appropriate for them at each stage. If operating from "old data" suppressed in the unconscious, suppressive foods may be chosen. This is a good area to us Aramaic Forgiveness Freedom Tools *[Part 2: MIND]* to move toward Lightening up. Listen to your Body-Mind, keep clearing out old content and toxins that want to "run the show" to discover a Lighter, more resilient you!

NOTE ON COFFEE AND STIMULANTS: Let's face it, as a modern culture we have a "coffee habit" difficult to walk away from. One reason coffee and cola beverages are so prevalent in our daily routine, is because high fat, high animal protein diet eventually destroys our natural enzymes needed for digestion, and we crave the acidity in these beverages to make digestion work. In this sense they are actually "medicinal." "Old thought data" that suppresses Life-force also invites stimulants. Wellness requires an alkaline Body, yet these beverages set up chronic acidity that can precede degeneration.

Coffee and cola beverages "push" our hormonal systems and Create acidity aggravating to the liver, making it difficult to stick with a raw, living foods or vegan diet. To enjoy a continually regenerative Lifestyle, commit to gradually withdrawing from anything but occasional coffee, benefits when eating heavier food. Decaf, espresso, French and cold pressed coffees are less acidic; also those produced without mold, organic and free-trade are "karma free." Even killing animals for food is a product of shadow blame-fear-hostility in the unconscious. Craving acidity and heavy foods expresses our burden of rage-fear-blame still in the suppressed in the unconscious causing acidic emotions.

Check our website for our additional books, videos, recipes, dietary transition chart *Climb the Transitional Ladder* and further accomplishing your Journey into greater Well-Being. It's nice to have guidance when we're getting started. For additional support, currently available on Amazon and Kindle by Cary Ellis: *Super Immunity Secrets - Fifty Vegan-Vegetarian Recipes & Immune Protective Herbs; Why Become a Vegetarian? Benefits for Health and Longevity; Truth About Weight Loss.*

DAILY CLEANSING ROUTINE - "SIMPLE RULES"

These "simple rules" are based on recovering healthy "leptin," the master hormone of the body that manages fat burning and keeping a lean, healthy metabolism.

1. BETWEEN MEALS - water - up to 4 quarts / day. Tea (coffee-min) - nothing added.

   a. Do not drink water at meals, instead drink 2 glasses 1/2 hour before meals. Studies have shown this helps with staying lean.

2. 3 MODERATE SIZE MEALS PER DAY (stomach size of two palms cupped)

3. 4-5 HRS. BETWEEN MEALS

4. 3 HRS. BETWEEN DINNER AND BED - NO FOOD

   a. If you feel the need to have something, make it a whole food. Herbal tea.

5. BREAKFAST CONTAINING PROTEIN or Low Glycemic foods

6. AVOID REFINED FOODS, WHITE FLOUR, WHITE SUGAR

7. LEAVE SOME WIGGLE ROOM 80/20 RULE - a "treat" now and then OK.

8. STICK WITH LOW GLYCEMIC FOODS (UNDER 55) [lists can be found online]

a. Examples

Low GI, 55 or less Examples include: legumes such as kidney, white, black, pink, soybeans; nuts   (almonds, peanuts, walnuts, chickpeas), and Seeds (sunflower, flax, pumpkin, poppy, sesame); most fruits (peaches, strawberries, mangos), most vegetables (beets, squash, parsnips); most whole intact grains (durum, spelt, kamut wheat, millet, oat, rye, rice, barley).

Medium GI, 56–69 Examples include: pita bread, basmati rice, potato, grape juice, raisins, prunes, pumpernickel bread, cranberry juice, regular ice cream, sucrose, and banana.

High GI, 70 and above Examples include: white bread, most white rice, corn flakes, most breakfast cereals, potato, and pretzels.

drpielet.com/3-things-you-can-do-today-to-start-losing-weight/

DAILY CLEANSING ROUTINE - BREAKFAST

1. **1 Qt. Warm Water a.m.** - Upon arising - warm or body temp water assists body
   1. plain or add a wedge or squeeze of fresh lemon or lime, or to alkalize - wedge of lime/lemon with pinch of baking soda (non-aluminum *Bob's*)
2. **TEA** (opt.) Herbal, black, green or white tea (no sweetener) Organic.
3. **COFFEE** Eliminate or reduce. If you're really hooked on coffee - have it after the above, try to stick to one cup per day or less. First Decaf then Espresso (home machine great) or cold press better than brewed - reduces acid; decaf also better. Organic. Fair Trade. Mold-free. Become a tea drinker!

NOTE: Yogic tradition of ***cleansing the stomach and intestines on awakening*** is long honored and beneficial. During the night we fast., after moderate dinner the evening before preferably 2-4 hrs before bed. During the night the stomach is empty, and by morning the body is ready to flush out waste products the organs and cells eliminated during the night. Up to a quart of warm water plain or with lemon-lime, is a wonderful routine first thing a.m.! :) It Lightens the body; clean feeling.

Daily practices clear Body-Mind-Spirit (previous section), burn incense, uplifting music, focus, meditate, pray in preparation for the Day; or as our Native American brother, John Woolf does, express three things you are Grateful for; as Ram Dass said, "Be Here Now..." connect with unlimited Creation from the *Field.*

LIGHT SUSTENANCE: We've supported our cleanse of the night with a Morning Flush. Our body appreciates us being gentle on our digestive system, breaking our night's "fast" with lighter fare, such as Smoothie or Green Shake. These are so popular they are available almost anywhere. Be sure to check ingredients to avoid refined sugar. Make at home with fresh ingredients (below), a great habit to cultivate; potent, regenerative Light nourishment! Making your own ensures your Smoothie or Green Shake is made from the best ingredients, and just right for you. Blend or shake, or just stir in a cup when traveling.

1. Smoothie or Green Shake - Light Sustenance (Recipe at end of chapter)
2. Follow with or have on alternate days heavier breakfast of choice
    a. Essene or Sprouted Grain Bread - Toast - Coconut Oil or avocado (opt.)
    b. Whole or sprouted grain tortilla - nut butter
    c. Raw Meuseli Cereal (rolled oats, raisins, nuts, coconut, nut milk) soak
    d. Potatoes / toast - If eating eggs or tofu - option

DAILY CLEANSING ROUTINE - LUNCH

Experiment with wholesome light Recipes at our site SuperImmunitySecrets.com

• Soups
• Salads
• Sandwiches, Sprouted Grain Breads or Tortillas
• Favorite PROTEINS

Francis Moore Lappé's 1971 bestselling *Diet for a Small Planet* and her subsequent books are foundational resources for how to meet protein needs on a vegan-vegetarian diet. Another tremendous resource is John Robbins (author of *Diet for a new America* and many more) *May All Be Fed: a Diet For A new World : Including Recipes By Jia Patton And Friends* with 200 awesome recipes. *(Cary worked a little with Jia Patton and EarthSave years ago in early stages of this book).*

• Beans and Peas such as black, great northern, white, navy, lentils, garbanzos, mung, adzuki *(sprout or soak and cook)*
• Grains such as quinoa and amaranth for balanced high protein
• Decrease animal products to less days per week or smaller quantities

• Fermented foods such as Kimchee or Raw Sauerkraut keep enzyme levels up

• Baked or stir-fried veggies

• International foods often contain great combinations of legumes and grains with vegetables and choice of no animal protein: Chinese, Mexican, Vietnamese, Mediterranean, Middle Eastern, Ethiopian, Thai and more...

DAILY CLEANSING ROUTINE - DINNER

Similar pattern to Lunch - with your (and your family's) favorite combos. Make dinner either same size or smaller than lunch; based on the principle that we cleanse overnight, allowing the system to rest. Our stomach is about the same size as our two palms cupped together; this is accurate for any size person or pet - based on their hands (or paws) and how much food intake is appropriate.

DAILY CLEANSING ROUTINE - 1 DAY FAST/week

It has been a practice of many we know on the path, to go without food or switch to Juices or All Raw one day per week. Whatever current Lifestyle style habits, it's a great experience to spend one day a week with Lighter intake, and also dedicate this day to thought-emotional clearing and "goal canceling;" framing new and realistic goals, developing our "purpose;" reading or dr. michael ryce video-audio (whyagain.org) or our videos, deepen the Journey, "develop new brain cells."

DAILY CLEANSING ROUTINE - NOTES

1. Yes you may make more trips to the bathroom. Be thankful that which no longer belongs is leaving. Drink less in evening. Keep water next to bed in case thirsty.

2. Bowel movements should occur at least once every 24 hours, supported by water drinking and fiber. Become familiar with your own bowel "transit time:" Eat beets or take charcoal tablets, which show up in stools as red or black. Support your Body rhythms, using the following to support healthy transit time and easy elimination.

• 1-2 tsp/day ground or soaked flax, psyllium husks, chia seed (rotate flax as it is a healthy food, thought daily use can Create GLA deficiency) good in shake

• Herbal Laxative - prefer blend with *cascara sagrada* over *senna* when needed

• Healthy gut bacteria is super-important, destroyed by antibiotics and meds. Restore w/probiotics (health food store), and regular use of raw cultured foods.

NOTE ON CLEANSES: Below are outlines of cleanses. Do your research, listen to your body. A cleanse is a personal choice. Consider weight, toxicity, how current habits differ from cleanse protocol. *Middle path is wisdom*; moderation in all things. Mix-and-match routines. These basics have worked for us well over many years (videos at our website).

DETOX: Add herbs, essential oils, with special focus and bodywork to cleanse/detox a particular organ/ tissue, or remove residues from the body.

GUIDED CLEANSES: It is good to have a buddy with whom you can exchange notes with who is familiar with cleansing. If you have not done a cleanse or feel you have an overload of toxins, seek out practitioners or a residential program to experience a cleanse the first time. Many programs such as wheatgrass institutes teach how to use enemas, colonics and wheatgrass implants, which can accelerate the body's cleansing process.

3 DAY CLEANSE (1x/month or every other)

TRUE ARAMAIC FORGIVENESS - Freedom Tool *[Part 2: MIND] 3-5/day*

Follow instructions (this chapter):
CLEANSING OUR VESSEL - DAILY PRACTICES FOR MIND & HEART

DAILY ROUTINE

"*1 Qt. Warm Water a.m.*" instructions under *Daily Cleansing Routine Breakfast*

    a. warm water with pinch of baking soda and wedge of lemon

    b. enjoy tea - let go of coffee for these 3 days

    c. drink 2-4 qts water and/or herbal tea during day between meals

DAY 1:

    a. Green Shake or Smoothie - Breakfast

    b. Salad with Steamed or Baked Veggies Lunch

    c. Fresh, Raw Vegetable Juices or Raw Blended Veggie Soup - Dinner

    d. Herbal Laxative, 1 tsp Ground Golden Flax or Psyllium Husks in glass water

DAY 2:

    a. Green Shake or Smoothie -Breakfast

    b. Fresh, Raw Vegetable Juices or Raw Blended Veggie Soup - Lunch

    c.Raw Salad - Dinner

    d. Herbal Laxative, 1 tsp Ground Golden Flax or Psyllium Husks in glass water

DAY 3:

    a. Fresh, Raw Vegetable Juices or Raw Blended Veggie Soup - Bkfst

    b. Fresh, Raw Vegetable Juices or Raw Blended Veggie Soup - Lunch

    c. Raw Salad and Vegan Soup cooked or raw - Dinner

    d. Herbal Laxative, 1 tsp Ground Golden Flax or Psyllium Husks in glass water

    Y*ay! You did it! Enjoy your Lightness and sticking to Lighter foods!*

7 DAY CLEANSE (1x spring- 1x fall)

TRUE ARAMAIC FORGIVENESS - Freedom Tool *[Part 2: MIND] 3-5/day*

Follow instructions daily (this chapter):
CLEANSING OUR VESSEL - DAILY PRACTICES FOR MIND & HEART

DAILY ROUTINE

"1 Qt. Warm Water a.m." instructions under *Daily Cleansing Routine Breakfast*

    a. warm water with pinch of baking soda and wedge of lemon

    b. enjoy tea - let go of coffee for these 3 days

    c. drink 2-4 qts water and/or herbal tea during day between meals

DAY 1: Same as DAY 1 - 3 Day Cleanse

DAY 2: Same as DAY 2 - 3 Day Cleanse

DAYS 3-4:

    a. Green Shake or Smoothie - Breakfast

    b.Fresh, Raw Vegetable Juices or Raw Blended Veggie Soup - Lunch

    c.Fresh, Raw Vegetable Juices - Dinner 1-3 cups

    d.Herbal Laxative, 1 tsp Ground Golden Flax or Psyllium Husks in glass water

DAY 5: *(trade shake or smoothie for 1 juice meal)*

    a.Fresh, Raw Vegetable Juices - Breakfast 1-3 cups

    b.Fresh, Raw Vegetable Juices - or Raw Blended Veggie Soup - Lunch

    c.Fresh, Raw Vegetable Juices - Dinner 1-3 cups

    d.Herbal Laxative, 1 tsp Ground Golden Flax or Psyllium Husks in glass water

DAY 7:

    a. Same as DAY 2 - 3 Day Cleanse

DAY 7:

    a. Green Shake or Smoothie -Breakfast

    b. Salad with Steamed or Baked Veggies Lunch

    c. Raw Salad and Vegan Soup - Dinner

    d. Herbal Laxative, 1 tsp Ground Golden Flax or Psyllium Husks in glass water

30 DAY CLEANSE (opt. 1x/yr)

TRUE ARAMAIC FORGIVENESS - Freedom Tool [Part 2: MIND] 3-5/day

Follow instructions daily (this chapter):

CLEANSING OUR VESSEL - DAILY PRACTICES FOR MIND & HEART

DAILY ROUTINE

"1 Qt. Warm Water a.m." instructions under *Daily Cleansing Routine Breakfast*

    e. warm water with pinch of baking soda and wedge of lemon

    f. enjoy tea - let go of coffee for these 3 days

    g. drink 2-4 qts water and/or herbal tea during day between meals

DAYS 1-30:

    a. Adapt patterns established in 3 DAY and 7 DAY Cleanses. Create your own "mix-and-match" based on:

        a. current lifestyle

b. whether you have time to "retreat" or are doing this during normal work - home week

c. if current nutrition has been a bit heavy or if dealing with illness, disease, or sensitivities - go gently

d. One option is to do several repeats of the 7DAY and end with the 3 DAY, or whatever adaptation fits.

21st Century Superhuman
GREEN SHAKE & SMOOTHIE RECIPES
more recipes at SuperImmunitySecrets.com

SMOOTHIES AND GREEN 98SHAKES: Mix and match from this general list, based on what you have available and suits your taste and phase of dietary transition. Shop at your local health food store, natural foods section at your grocery store, local organic grower or order online. There are awesome online and offline resources for live Superfoods. Measurements are for 1 shake. All ingredients and measurements are variable to taste. GENERAL RECIPE:

LIQUID 2 cups Water with Nut, Coconut, Rice Milk. If you buy pre-made, get without sugar. Make your own, blend soaked nuts-seeds with water.

GREENS - 1-2 Tbs Wheatgrass, Barleygrass, Other Mixed Grass Powders; Spirulina - Excellent Protein Source; Chlorella - a must for detoxing mercury; Blue Green Algae; Supergreen Blends (several excellent available); Ormus Supergreens (Sunwarrior)

FIBER 1-3 tsp
Psyllium Husks, Ground Flax - golden (preferable), Soaked Whole Flax

PROTEIN 1-2 T Vegan Protein Powder; raw soaked nuts-seed

FRUIT Fresh, Frozen, Dried, preferably organic; Frozen bananas thicken

SUPERFOODS Many popular exotic - try out different things and find out what you like Cacao, Carob, Maca, Gogi Berry, Ginseng, Bilberry, Bee Pollen

NUTS OR SEEDS Chia Seed, Hemp Seed, Coconut, Raw Nuts or Seeds (soaked)
Soak overnight to start sprouting process and make "living food"

SPICES: Cinnamon. Coriander, Ginger

FRESH GREENS & VEGGIES: Kale, cucumber, apple, ginger, broccoli, spinach, etc.

21st Century Superhuman GREEN SHAKE

NOTE: Rotate items for variety. Enjoy in a.m. & save in fridg for later, or make more and share with household. NOTE: Can also be savory shake without fruit. Blend in blender with 2-4 cups water:

•1/2 cup Frozen Organic fruit, 1/2 banana, 1/2-1 fresh apple (choice or blend)

• 1/2-1 tsp. Spirulina; 1/2-1 tsp. Chlorella; 1/2-1 tsp. blue-green algae (choice or blend)

•1-2 tsp Ormus Supergreens (build up to it); 2 tsp Wheatgrass/Barleygrass Powder

•1 T Supergreen Powder Blend: *Pure Synergy* , *Vitamineral Green* or blend with probiotics

• 1 T Hemp Seed (whole); 1 T Chia Seed (whole) - can soak overnight

• 2 T Soaked (whole) or ground Golden Flaxseed (include walnuts or hemp for Omega 6)

• 1 T Vegan Protein Powder (opt) favorites: Sunwarrior & Garden of Life

• Fresh organic greens such as spinach or kale; Moranga powder (40% protein leaf)

>   With veggies and no fruit: opt. cayenne, ginger, garlic, cumin, curry

21st Century Superhuman SMOOTHIE

A Smoothie provides quick, easy nutritious, delicious substantive meal that can carry us for hours. Fun and delicious! Blend in blender:

• 2 cups favorite Milk Alternative (nut, seed, coconut, almond, hemp, hazelnut, soy)

• Dilute with a little water (opt). Can make own nut/seed milk w/water & flavor.

• 1/2 cup Frozen Fruit / frozen banana with other fruit thickens (or use no fruit)

• If sweeter desired, add a couple of dates or dash maple syrup

• 1-2 T Vegan Protein Powder - favorites: Sunwarrior, Garden of Life, Ultimate Meal

Optional additions:

• 1 tsp green powder blend (see Green Shake - any combo)

• 1/2 tsp cacao, vanilla, cinnamon, ginger, coriander, carob

• gogi berries, maca or other favorite superfood

• 1 tsp hempseed, chia seed, flaxseed (soaked or ground)

• (include walnuts or hemp for Omega 6 to balance flax)

RAW BLENDED VEGGIE SOUP: 2-3 cups water, cut up raw organic veggies seasonal, greens, tomatoes, cucumbers, garlic, cruciferous, lemon juice, sea salt, cayenne herbs, spices, tamari, umeboshi plum.

THINK GREEN: In Ancient Egypt Green was used for healing. Chlorophyll and hemoglobin are identical, except hemoglobin has iron at the center of the molecule, and chlorophyll has magnesium. Blood cleanses and rebuilds quickly with dark green. Wheatgrass juice has many testimonials to this. Wheatgrass juice and green powders purify the blood, and clean out eliminative organs, open channels of elimination. If flu-like symptoms occur, increase fluids and support better elimination (enemas, herbs, implants).

WHEATGRASS: Without having to grow your own wheatgrass, stir into water daily excellent dehydrated wheatgrass juice powders.

CATCH OUR VIDEOS - at YouTube and at our website easy cleansing-detox "how to's."

Part 4: BODY
Chapter 8
Nature's Simplest Remedies

Deprive a cell of 35% of its oxygen for 48 hours and it may become cancerous.

Dr. Otto H. Warburg (1883-1970)
Nobel Prize Medicine 1931, Nominated Nobel Prize Physiology 1944

Mother Nature is simple; when we understand how she works and plays, we align with the grandest, most Innate power there is. Simple basic principles and practices hold the *Field* for health, well-being and vitality. There is peace in knowing we are One with All That Is. Aligning Mind-Heart with LOVE and clearing ALL thought-emotion Not of LOVE, is our first step, then according to Universal Law we discover resources within nature that kindly nurture and help correct our imbalances.

> Everything is energy and that's all there is to it. Match the frequency of the reality you want and you cannot help but get that reality. It can be no other way. This is not philosophy. This is physics.

Albert Einstein (1879-1955)
Theory or Relativity, Nobel Prize Physics 1921, Max Planck Medal 1929

It is amazing how once we become confident of the direction we are going, how much our Lifestyle changes, and just a few simple remedies can give us a feeling of comfort and relief. Remember: the body's movement is *always* toward wellness. Any typical symptom that might be considered cold, flu, coughing, sneezing, nausea, vomiting, diarrhea, and even degenerative conditions, are generally efforts of the body to cleanse and Lighten up!

Critical to physical well-being is that cells and tissues require oxygen, as demonstrated by Nobel Laureate Dr. Otto Warburg in 1924. Simplest natural remedies help clear away acidity, inflammation and toxicity, restoring oxygenation to the cells. When access to oxygen is blocked because of cellular congestion, cells become anaerobic and fermentation occurs. Nature uses her best efforts to clean-up where the flow of Life Force is blocked, with these typical acute symptoms of cleansing.

> Cancer, above all other diseases, has countless secondary causes. But, even for cancer, there is only one prime cause. Summarized in a few words, the prime cause of cancer is the replacement of the respiration of oxygen in normal body cells by a fermentation of sugar [or anaerobic condition].
>
> *Dr. Otto H. Warburg (1883-1970)*
> *Nobel Prize Medicine 1931, Nominated Nobel Prize Physiology 1944*

Health, holy, holistic and whole come from the same Indo-European root word (6-7,000 years ago), to be healthy is to be whole is to be holy. When Life Force flows to us continually from the ever-creating *Field* we are well and whole. If this flow of Life Energy and oxygen is blocked dis-ease results.

Where does this flow being blocked begin? Mind-Energy Not of LOVE. As a result of this thought-emotion the the system becomes overloaded with too much, too heavy, too rich, toxic substances, and the flow of Life Force slows. Toxins crystalize in tissues and cells, acidity, inflammation, fibrins and free radicals reduce oxygen levels and stimulate development of layers of mucous for buffering. So toxemia begins. Fasting, cleansing and goal canceling remove unconscious Mind-Energy. This is when it's nice to have simple remedies to assist.

When we have accumulated enough toxic waste in our system and eliminative organs from heavier and richer foods, in greater quantity than the body needs, it has no choice but to cleanse, which we call illness. Statistically those who become vegan, vegetarian and eat lightly, are much less prone to illness. The fastest, most efficient and lasting way to remove symptoms when they do show up, is by changing our internal ecosystem; juicing, fasting, cleansing and restoring balance to the gut with probiotics.

FURTHER READING: Dr. Sircus.com: on baking soda, magnesium chloride and iodine is very informative. Founder, International Medical Veritas Association (IMVA), he cites these remedies as primary to keep us well in today's World; *excellent resource.*

Baking Soda - Best Friend

Optimally we maintain healthy alkalinity through low-fat, high percentage raw, vegan-vegetarian foods, green shakes, juices, water, cleansing and clear Mind-Heart. However modern lifestyle results in inflammation due to stress and poor diet, with resulting acidity and overload of toxemia, laying the foundation for degenerative dis-ease.

Our body is like an alkaline battery, much more power, endurance and running best when it is in alkaline balance. Oxygen to the cells is a critical factor. So if our bodies are in overload, in order to relieve our discomfort we seek cleansing and alkalization. The long term answer builds this into our Lifestyle. Alkalizing water machines can also support alkalinity. Primary is learning about alkaline lifestyle from foods, soil and incorporating.

Regular small pinches of baking soda in water can assist in restoring alkaline pH to the body, while at the same time we clear thoughts, cleanse and detox, while transitioning to more alkaline nutrition. A tiny pinch of (non-aluminum such as Bob's) baking soda in water in the morning assists with neutralizing acidity.

Teddi's experience with Dr. Stone: Teddi spent many years taking environmentally sensitive clients for treatment with Dr. Stone. A client going through a panic attack when they walked in the door, was handed a small cup half-full of a clear liquid. The client drank it down with symptoms of panic or allergy instantly relieved. "What was it?" they asked. It was "baking soda and water." Powerful, simple support for many "crisis" situations.

Testing *pH*: For accuracy, one can obtain pH test paper at a pharmacy. Optimal pH range is 6.5 to 7.2. Test saliva or clean stream of urine first thing in a.m. Baking soda more or less often can help maintain ph level. Eventually you will learn what it feels like to be alkaline.

First aid: In the case of anything that itches or burns, where the body is activating a histamine reaction, such as stings, bites or poison ivy or oak, a sip of baking soda internally and application externally support the body in relief of symptoms.

Baking Soda for cancer: Dr. Simoncini oncologist in Italy uses sodium bicarbonate intravenously to reverse cancer successfully. Dr. Sircus relates that taking baking soda internally and soaking in baths is equal to Dr. Simoncini's IV treatments.

Stories of cancer reversal with Baking Soda (online): One man cured himself of cancer by using baking soda with molasses. The sweetness carries the baking soda into the cell and helps the cell become alkaline, acting like a Trojan horse. Another young woman who had four sisters who died of breast cancer, when questioned as to what she thought was different about herself, said she sipped on water with baking soda and maple syrup daily; similarly to gentleman above. (See his videos online "Run From the Cure")

Colds -Flu: Dr. Sircus encourages a daily combination of baking soda, magnesium chloride and iodine to prevent any symptoms of cold of flu during winter seasons. We include with that the benefits of cleansing and Living on Lighter nutrition to Create a foundational clean Body honored as the *"House We Live In."* Food grown in mineralized soils does a great deal to keep us more alkaline.

Magnesium Chloride

Magnesium deficiency is rampant in the modern diet, with excess refined grains and sugars. Demineralization of soils and non-organic foods have also greatly reduced magnesium levels in foods. Common Epsom Salts boost magnesium levels, though does not last long. Dr. Sircus recommends the use of transdermal magnesium chloride as the most effective way to improve magnesium levels quickly.

Magnesium is an Essential Mineral used for hundreds of biochemical reactions, making it crucial for health. Massive magnesium deficiencies in the general population have led to a tidal wave of sudden coronary deaths, diabetes, strokes and cancer. Even a mild deficiency of magnesium can cause increased sensitivity to noise, nervousness, irritability, mental depression, confusion, twitching, trembling, apprehension, and insomnia.

Dr. Sircus, Dr Sircus.com

We use his recommended magnesium chloride from an ancient seabed, just a pinch in our water in the morning, and foot soaks with excellent results. Dr. Sircus suggests use of these 3 inexpensive, self-treatable natural substances, for supporting renewal of equilibrium of the body; baking soda, magnesium chloride and transdermal iodine. He suggests a high quality iodine - easily rub a bit into skin of forearm rather than internally.

Epsom Salts

Readily available: Epsom salts can be easily and inexpensively found at any pharmacy. S form of magnesium obtainable if a person does not have access to Ancient seabed magnesium chloride. Used externally for foot soaks and baths, Epsom salts assist the body to shift to an alkaline state and can relieve tension and cramping. Dr. Sircus recommends both baking soda and magnesium for cardio and cancer, two leading de-generative conditions in the modern World. Epsom salt soak or foot soak when feeling stressed, over-tired or toxic can be beneficial, however the magnesium is not retained long in this form.

Hydrotherapy: Simply getting into a tub of warm water is an old form of hydrotherapy, drawing congestion from the trunk of the body, rebalancing the body's energy flows in a gentle way. Using Epsom salts along with a warm bath can be very supportive of improving one's state of well-being, or simply a warm-hot bath alone assists body balance.

Diatomaceous Earth

A fossil of ancient algae: Diatomaceous earth is a naturally occurring fossilized rock that crumbles into a fine white powder, called "fossil shell flour." It can be slightly abrasive and is highly porous. It is commonly used for filtration, in gardens, sometimes in toothpaste, and is a mechanical insecticide, shredding the gut of the insect that ingests it. Engineer, Wilhelm Berkefeld recognized its ability to filter, and developed tubular filters (known as filter candles) fired from diatomaceous earth, successfully used in the1892 cholera epidemic in Germany.

Because diatomaceous earth occurs naturally in various deposits, different "mines" contain various minerals not for internal consumption. Perma-guard, mines and seels "animal food grade" diatomaceous earth, approved for the consumption of animals. Diatomaceous earth is hollow with negatively charged spaces that draw toxins or positively charged ions such as heavy metals out of the body.

Founder and former president of Perma-Guard, Wally Tharp passed away at the ripe age of 89, after 52 years of spreading information about use of diatomaceous earth. When I (Cary) met him he was 80, with a spring in his step and the brightest blue eyes I had ever seen. He told me he been taking a teaspoon a day of diatomaceous earth for 30 years, besides which he lived a committed healthy Lifestyle. I've always attributed the brightness of his eyes to the regular pulling of toxins with the diatomaceous earth.

Perma-guard diatomaceous earth is a great non-toxic insecticide, for home, garden and on pets for fleas. Internally for animals it has been found to do no harm and in tests run where animals took it for five years it kept away bacteria and parasites. Wally told a story of two sheep with brucellosis a serious bacterial illness, next to each other; one was given diatomaceous earth in its food and was alive the next morning, the other did not survive.

Diatomaceous earth is used for filtering pool water, this one could be used for filtering water on camping trips or outside the normal system. It is it an excellent resource to replace insecticides that might be used around home, pets or garden, with a non-toxic substance supportive of human health. The greatest precaution, as Wally used to tell us, is just to be careful not to inhale it! I like carrying a supply on camping trips and into the wilderness.

Activated Charcoal

Activated Charcoal is an old-time remedy: It probably goes back to the stone age. We've never tried chewing on a stick of wood burned to black char out of the fire pit, but the right wood would do, in an emergency. Videos online explain how to make your own charcoal with traditional time-honored methods, going back historically in many cultures. It would be fun and useful to try out and make homemade charcoal.

We generally purchase what is called activated (oxygen added) charcoal tablets or capsules at the health food store, considering it an important item for our *"natural first aid kit."* Charcoal is commonly used for poisoning or snake venom because it draws or *adsorbs* hundreds of times its volume, meaning it attracts or magnetizes particles holding them like a magnet to be carried away.

Activated charcoal tablets or caps are an excellent resource, commonly used for stomach gas or indigestion, and have been shown to reduce diarrhea in cancer patients. Charcoal biscuits were sold in England in the early 19th century for gas and stomach troubles. Activated charcoal is used in acute poisoning, and has also been found to remove pesticide residue from the body. It is a great addition to a cleanse for elimination of heavy metals, mercury and pesticides. Carbon removes chlorine and other impurities in home water filtration, but does not remove fluoride. (Do NOT use prepared charcoal for the grill internally, as it often contains chemicals).

Flower Remedies

Flower Remedies are low potency homeopathic solutions made from flowers and plants, to harmonize and balance the emotional body. Edward Bach had a gift for developing these gentle flower remedies, by putting blossoms in a clean glass bowl in water in the sunlight to extract their essence. "...They cure not by attacking the dis-ease, but by flooding our bodies with beautiful Vibrations of our higher nature, in the presence of which disease melts away as snow in the sunshine. There is no true healing unless there is a change in outlook, peace of mind, and inner happiness."

> All fear must be cast out; it should never exist in the human mind...The cause of all our troubles is self and separateness, and this vanishes as soon as LOVE and the knowledge of the great Unity become part of our natures. ... A person's body is the objective manifestation of his internal nature; he is the expression of himself, the materialization of the qualities of his consciousness.

Edward Bach 1886-1936
The Bach Flower Remedies

Flower essences can be obtained from natural health suppliers or online, with books available, and numerous flower essences produced by gifted Beings. Enjoy Lightening Body-Mind-Heart, support your movement into Higher thought-emotional Frequencies with emotional clearing. RESOURCES: The Bach Centre, La Vie de la Rose Flower Essences

Essential Oils

In Ancient times Essential Oils were valued as it takes much of a natural substance to produce the oils. Several companies make high quality oils and offer amazing combinations anti viral-fungal-bacterial and supportive of Well-Being. This is an entire field of study, so do your research, learn which ones you are drawn to and use regularly. They're addicting!

Herbs and Spices - Super Immunity Secrets

We LOVE herbs and spices fresh and dried! Senses respond in a kitchen where food is being prepared with herbs and spices. We hunger for scents, frequencies and energies that herbs and spices bring into our lives. It's easy to learn how to add herbs and spices to dishes both hot and cold, saturating the dish with super micro-nutrients and subtle miraculous, nurturing, healing qualities. It is said that plants foods when taken into the body actually communicate with and harmonize energy in the cells.

Cary's book, *Super Immunity Secrets*, available on Amazon and Kindle, contains 175 clinical references on herbs and spices, and 50 vegan-vegetarian recipes enriched by these nourishing elements. Once you have a few herbs blessing your kitchen, you won't ever be without them. Growing them in your garden, or in pots around the house is a wonderful addition to a healthy home, as are the fresh supplies of dried bulk herbs and spices obtainable at your local health food store or co-op.

Herbs and spices contain some of the deepest neurological links for our DNA coding, connecting us to literally thousands of years of humanity walking in Earth-Wisdom, flowing with the seasons living in harmony with the natural World. Herbs bring us subtle messages through energies of nature, Earth Mother Gaia and plant elementals.

Spices and herbs contain micronutrients, and even their scents offer gifts to the body. They evolved through natural selection over thousands of years. They offer potentized intrinsic Life elements, that cannot be identified in a laboratory. They bring eternal gifts for the Body when they bless us with their presence. Treasure your sources, your plant cuttings, seeds and starts to be shared with friends, family and community.

Here is a quick sampling:

Cilantro *detoxes mercury* - add to soups, salads. Cilantro Pesto - grind together in food processor: 1 bunch cilantro, 1 bunch parsley, 5-6 cloves garlic, salt, lemon, 1/-2 - 1 cup walnuts or pine nuts, 1/2 cup olive oil, dash lemon or lime juice. Yum! Have on toast, sandwiches, salads or by the spoon. Great detoxifier.

Garlic *natural anti-biotic, contains allicin* - very similar to Penicillin. Use in soups, salads, sandwiches and salad dressings. Teddi's grandkids love slices of raw garlic on crackers during "cold" season. Chlorophyll or parsley helps take away the garlic smell, as does peppermint. As a more "sociable" resort, garlic capsules offer some of the elements of raw garlic.

Garlic is high in selenium: decreases toxic affects of fluoride and mercury binds with them; assists with glutathione production and the conversion of T4 to T3 supporting healthy thyroid function. Selenium supports healthy DNA, keeps unhealthy molecules from reproducing, inhibits tumor growth and causes death of cancerous and precancerous cells. Positive effects increase when taken with iodine. Metal Detox: garlic-cilantro juice with chlorella

Ginger - Supports digestion, add fresh to soups, stir-fry, smoothies, juices

Turmeric - Shown to be as *effective anti-inflammatory* as Hydrocortisone. Warm up in almond or coconut milk for an evening beverage.

Medical Marijuana - Successfully used in cancer treatment pets and people

ACTIVATE NEW FREQUENCIES: Herbs and spices subtly help remove layering, and bring Higher Frequencies to our physical vehicle with micro-nutrition. These are true gifts of the natural World, that smooth out our neurobiological response to Life, making our transit through things that come up happen with greater ease.

Probiotics

Probiotics are essential microorganisms, naturally found in a healthy intestinal track. Once we have taken antibiotics (against life) even once, we kill off the most beneficial, and it is important to repopulate them. Bifidus is the bacteria found in the gut in infancy, killed off when a first antibiotic is taken. Get to know and use raw cultured foods such as sauerkraut, kimchee, miso, yogurt, kombucha, natural pickles and more; also capsules and liquids can be found at health food suppliers. Repopulate healthy bacteria in the gut for wellness and protection of well-being. The are a key subtle factor within the body that assists us to fight illness and stay well. One young mother we know keeps probiotics capsules in the house, and when anyone in her family is fighting off a cold or sickness, she loads them up with probiotics, supporting the body's natural immunity.

Food Grade Hydrogen Peroxide, MMS, Colloidal Silver

Food grade hydrogen peroxide was first used in 1920 by IV to successfully treat a pneumonia epidemic. In the 1940's Father Richard Willhelm, pioneer in promoting peroxide use, reported on it being used to treat everything from bacterial-related mental illness to skin disease and polio. It has been used successfully for cancer and a list of other illness. Its effectiveness has to do with its extra molecule of oxygen.

Food grade hydrogen peroxide 10-35% is purchased from health food suppliers. ALWAYS dilute before using as this concentration is dangerous. (Do not use drug store type as it contains additives not to be taken internally. Do not use hair products). Look up proper dilutions. Once diluted it can be used to support internal and external cleansing. Do your research before use. It is also used for disinfecting externally. Much information is available at numerous sites.

MMS is chlorine dioxide. Drops are mixed with citric acid to activate and diluted in water to drink. It has been used now to cure hundreds of cases of HIV, malaria, parasites and more. Jim Humble has spent many years working to educate on the value of MMS. His educational materials are very informative. MMS generally needs to be purchased in the U.S. as a water purifier. Do your research. This is a great and useful item to have on hand, excellent for traveling with exposure to microorganisms.

Colloidal silver is water that has been exposed to silver so retains the memory, frequency or small amount of silver in it. It is taken internally as an antibiotic, and is so potent it was used by the military to clean wounds in Afghanistan. Can be made o bought.

Restructuring Water

Natural water carries great Life-force for the body. This is a great way to restore charge to water that has traveled through pipes. Use a short piece of PVC pipe 8-12." Add another piece of pipe to cup over end, with added piece on bottom to Create a smaller outlet. Get non-toxic clear glass marbles and fill the pipe. This will allow the water to flow in vortex motions like eddies in current, mimic flow of nature through the marbles, creating a natural charge. Simply pour water through marbles in pipe into cup. Drink.

Sunshine, Solar Rays, Vitamin D3, Fresh Air

Who loves to be outdoors? We Are Solar Earth Beings. Get inspired to be outside whenever you can. Escape the indoor prison of our modern Lifestyle. If you live in a winter climate learn about and use Vitamins D3 and K2 (Jeff Bowles books), take a trip to warmer climes; photosynthesis with your skin. Solar energies on our bodies play a profound role in rejuvenating glandular function, supporting youthfulness and vitality. Raise your frequency with Solar Energy Now! Be Radiant! Smile! ♥

Chapter 9

Supportive Modalities

Once the power of frequency is understood,
it's easy to bring the body back to balance.
Happy cells are the body's equivalent to bliss.

Thomas Stone M.D.
Environmental Medicine

D o we understand yet that we are energy beings? It is a very big leap after so many eons of living and believing our World is simply mechanical parts, Now revealing we are made of energy. Even our bodies are made up of fast moving particles, our senses interpret as solid form yet constantly in motion.

As matter emerges from the *Field of Possibilities* it forms spinning atoms made of protons neutrons, electrons and smaller particles, leptons and quarks. As comprehension grows we view our World in an expanded way. Exciting remedial measures are emerging that support the Body by reading, engaging, adjusting and balancing its natural energetic electromagnetic systems.

These systems measure what is inhibiting or over-amping natural energy flow. Thinking we have an illness or that an illness is incurable, is a mis-understanding of how our Body operates. The question is, "How much are we willing to shift our thoughts and Lifestyle, and use supportive modalities to restore flow of Innate Creative energy without interruption, gifting us with wellness and vitality as our reward!

What we can Be, experience and do is slowed only by lingering old programs within us and associated habits. We are entering a new paradigm of human existence, breaking free from old conditioning, and growing into our potential to operate without limits forever! Our favorite *Remedial Measures* help us refresh our neurobiology, as we shed old layers of inhibiting thought-emotion. The first thing to ask ourselves when we're feeling sick, unwell, un-comfortable, or that dis-ease or de-generation is brewing, is to Leap into our "Greater Self," and ask self, "Self, where am I "shut down" on a physical, thought or emotional level? And how can I clear it quickly, easily?

> Between stimulus and response there is a space... In that space is our power to choose our response. In our response lies our growth and our freedom.
>
> *Dr. Viktor Frankl (1905-1997)*
> *Auschwitz Survivor, "Man's Search for Meaning"*

This can be a scary question (this is why we're dis-eased, because this information was so painful we shut it away in the first place), and we might not know how to unravel it. For this reason, wonderful remedial measures can help us regain and keep balance in our organism, while we're learning to clean out deeper content at cause. Old "corrupt data," carbon-based thought-emotion crystallizes in the body creating dis-comfort and dis-ease as a feedback mechanism. To dissolve the crystallization and free ourselves from its associated data we move through things we've likely been "stuck" in for years.

Tony Robbins taught us to use Pattern Interrupts to get out of being *Stuck!* This means exploring new ways to move out of "normal" mode. Surprise yourself, jump up-and-down or just Smile to access a new state of Being! As our physiology changes, our thought-emotional content shifts. Get out of being STUCK Now!!! Move! Breathe! Smile! Play with a friend, *Leap for Joy! Laugh!*

As we move out of our old "stuck" states, we can access greater clarity. We have the option to shape ourselves anew and choose to open up! It's vitally important to LOVE ourselves without judgment or expectation, with full self-acceptance just as we are. As William Shakespeare said, *"There is nothing good or bad but our thinking makes it so."* Upcoming remedial measures are of great assistance to move forward with deep clearing to bring Wellness and Vitality, shedding dis-integrative old patterns.

> I was very afraid at the beginning, until Master told me that pain isn't the truth; it's what you have to get through in order to find the truth.
>
> Deepak Chopra MD
> *The Return of Merlin*

There is no dark or light, no good or evil; *all there is is energy* and how we qualify it with our thought-emotion, conscious-unconscious Mind-Energy. We have the opportunity every moment, to step into a self healing, regenerative mode, where our cells wake up, spin faster and take out the "garbage" for vitality and well-being! *"Tell the truth quicker, have more fun per hour!"*

As long as we carry fear and hostility in Mind-Body structure, we crave things and express thoughts that bathe our tissues in acidic fluids, sustaining the state of fear or hostility crystallized in our cellular structure. It takes choice of "will" to to follow a "higher path" to let go ten thousand generations of blame-fear-hostility. The purpose of remedial measures is to ease and accelerate our restorative process.

Each individual practitioner has their own belief and method of expressing their craft. They may or may not fully "get" what you are learning here or they may (you can always introduce them to it). Seek out those who harmonize with your objectives. Learn what modalities work best for you. Different practitioners and methodologies will serve you better at different times, depending on your level of density or Lightness of Being. We offer short definitions here to assist you in finding helpful services to meet your needs. Do your own research of practitioners in your area to find those who are most supportive.

Breath Work

Conscious use of the Breath has been an active part of healing techniques for thousands of years. Simple relaxation and focusing on the Breath as a meditation in and of itself, gradually shifts us internally. During the last century Rebirthing and Holotropic Breath work were developed and became popular. They are most often practiced with a facilitator, to release holding patterns in Body-Mind.

Holding the Breath is a residual of blame-fear-hostility mode, usually learned in childhood, continuing until Attention is brought to it. dr. michael ryce developed Stillpoint which we do a version of in our programs, and he and his instructors do as well. Releasing through Breath with Stillpoint detaches layers of "corrupt data" from Body-Mind, conscious-unconscious, and supports us in entering an expanded state.

Placing Attention on clearing thought-emotion with our "goal canceling" processes, we Breathe through whatever comes up. It's important to note thought crystalized in Body goes through 3 stages while releasing: 1. solid crystals, 2. liquid - tears, 3 vapor - dissipates. Breathing through, rather than getting "stuck" in crying is helpful to move layers of old pain to be transmuted into vapor.

Breathing through the layers moves us through them much more quickly, rather than crying, which is a way to hold onto our resistance. Breathing helps us keep clearing the old "data banks" of the unconscious. In the Ancient Aramaic it says that when Yeshua-Jesus was with a crowd, he "Breathed them." With no context for what that meant, it was translated in the Bible as he "Breathed on them." dr. michael ryce's work with the Aramaic brings forward that Yeshua-Jesus "Breathed them," or taught them to Breathe, to release unconscious data in the true Aramaic Forgiveness process.

Breathe. Breathe. Breathe. Breathe...

Find a friend to support you in Breathing through things as they come up with your "goal canceling process," when layers surface. Breathing activates *Khooba* LOVE filter in the brain for *Perceptions*; Smiling activates *Rakhma* LOVE filter in the brain for our *Intentions*; important neurobiological reasons to Breathe and SMILE. [Part 2: MIND]

EFT - Emotional Freedom Technique or Tapping

EFT tapping is a very simple and effective method of rewiring our neurobiology, by tapping lightly with one's own fingertips on meridian points on head, face and more, while issues clear and new thoughts replace them. It's easy to learn how to do tapping on yourself, and it is also done by practitioners.

EFT tapping is beneficial to incorporate for anyone desiring greater clarity, well-being and empowerment. We make the biggest changes when we "free the resistance." This "rewiring" is important for the **21st Century Superhuman** toolbox to transform stored trauma and drama into positive and productive states.

This is an extremely powerful technology to utilize along with the Ancient Aramaic Forgiveness goal canceling processes to literally remove thousands of generations of "corrupt data," and then support re-wiring of our neural systems. As we clear our unconscious container of "old data" EFT tapping helps establish and sustain our new state of Being; beneficial to integrate into daily routine.

EFT has become very popular, with many easy tutorials online. Gary Craig developed EFT in the early 90's. A Stanford engineer, he trained in Dr. Roger Callahan's Thought Field Therapy or TFT, which became the father of EFT. They worked together with a woman client who was terrified of water. After doing tapping with her, she was instantly so unafraid she was willing to go swimming.

At www.emofree.com Gary (the originator's) free tutorials show how to do tapping yourself, with many other videos available as well such as Nick Ortner's Tapping Summit. Over five years of working with clients, Gary discovered that the sequence of tapping was basically irrelevant. He says, "Memories buried alive never die, they just show up in a bigger, uglier way." Robert Smith's FastEFT is also excellent, with instructions on YouTube.

Essential Oils and Aromatherapy

Essential oils and combinations are a fabulous addition to Healthy Lifestyle. Recent studies show that plant essences communicate with the cells of the body, interacting with them with Innate wisdom. Using essential oils on a regular basis is powerfully protective and beneficial. Also called Aromatherapy, essential oils shift body frequencies and assist it to clear, passing the blood-brain barrier and interacting with the body at subtle levels. Essential oils have been used for thousands of years as medicines, incense, insect repellent, perfume, antiseptic, anti-inflammatory, analgesic - pain relief, much proven scientifically in recent years. Undiluted oils are known as therapeutic grade and should be diluted with carrier oils. Dilute essential oils have been rubbed on baby's spines as young as a day old, and on mama's tummies before birth.

Aerial diffusion: fragrance; aerial disinfection; Vibrational clearing

Direct inhalation of scent: respiratory disinfection, decongestion, expectoration; psychological and neurobiological clearing and balancing

Topically in carrier oil: massage, body and energy work; baths, foot soaks, compresses and therapeutic skin care

Crystals, Gemstones, Gem Elixirs,

Once exposed to natural essential oils and their combinations, they become a fantastic addition to h

Bodywork: Massage, Feldenkrais, Rolfing, Reflexology, Point Holding, Acupressure, Hot Stone Massage, and more

In our modern culture it's easy to lose touch with the Body. Touch, and the comfort of bodywork can play an intrinsic role to restore health and well being. Good bodywork is extremely healing, and most of us could give and receive more. The soothing comfort of touch from friend, family member or practitioner, can assist with letting go of layers with ease, through both bodywork and energy work.

Wonderful styles of body work have evolved, that help restore balance, equilibrium and connectedness within the Body. Some swear by "their form of bodywork," which just shows the difference between bodies and individual needs. If you are drawn to a practitioner and a particular style of massage or bodywork, and can afford it, enjoy the regular therapy of receiving; in fact signing up for regular sessions or a series can produce deep and long-lasting results.

There are great techniques to good massage, yet most of us have an innate sense of the Body, when we allow ourselves. Access your sensitivity by working on someone else and letting intuition direct. Trading with a friend and giving each other feedback assists us to grow in this important art. Massage and energy work do not necessarily have a sexual connotation although they are used with Ancient Tantra. They are wonderful tools through which we assist one another in our personal, physical-spiritual Evolution, removing old layers that no longer serve and vitalizing Joyful Being.

Owning a massage table shared between several, is a fine resource for exchanging bodywork and energy balancing. Learning as you go is supportive of inner healing for both giver and receiver. Add essential oils, Breathwork and energy balancing for an extraordinary experience. This is also a wonderful nurturing exchange between partners in a relationship, with agreement as to what focus to take. Massage and energy work can easily be done as an exchange between friends. There are hundreds of types of massage, descriptions available online. To become a practitioner be sure to check with regulations in your area.

"Energy Medicine:" Acupuncture, Reiki, Polarity, Crystals, Qi-Gong, Chakra Balancing, Meridian Healing, Matrix Energetics, Sound Healing, Crystal Bowls, Gongs, Tai Chi, Martial Arts and more

"Energy Medicine" emerged with the Indus Valley civilization around 3,500 B.C. and fed out into many cultures and practices in the Eastern World, China, India, Japan, Asia, Tibet and more. Acupuncture, Vedic system, Qi-Gong, Chakras, Gongs, Chanting, Reiki and other energy balancing practices care for the body as an energy vehicle, with energetic pathways not perceived by modern medicine in the West.

The various arts of energy medicine are extremely effective, non-invasive, supporting the body in regaining balance so it can continue with its movement towards wellness. Most of them include dietary practices predominantly toward vegetarian. Several recognize emotions being stored in the unconscious with practices for clearing.

Certain forms of energy work are done with hands off the body or lightly touching to activate, balance, energize, shift and move energy *Fields*. Again, we all have the ability to sense energy *Fields* in and around the body and can learn to support them, by working on one another, apprenticing or following our intuition.

In Lynn McTaggart's book, *"The Field"* she reminds us that *everyone*, even those who don't think they do, have intuitive sensitivities. As we learn to exchange healing touch and support, it can be bonding among community, friends or family, and nurturing and healing to all.

It is relatively easy these days to locate practitioners or teachers of Acupuncture, Qi-gong, Reiki, Crystal Bowls and more. Participating in groups who use gongs chanting and movement is a great way to cultivate energy enhancing practices.

Yoga - Hatha, Kundalini, Ashtanga, Bikram, Hot, Iyengar, Vinyasa, more

Although physical yoga popularized in the modern World, might be "exercise," it is also essentially a therapeutic blending of Body-Mind-Heart-Spirit with the goal of raising consciousness, emerging from thousands of years of highly evolved Ancient Tradition. Indus Valley Civilization dating to 3,500 B.C.E. depicted figures in yoga or meditation poses on clay tablets. Emerging current views on "reality," align with more with these inherited Ancient Teachings than with recent science.

Yoga is designed to keep Body and Breath flowing, activating energy pathways, glands and chakras, by objectifying Enlightenment, through clarifying the physical form to reflect more Light. Many yogic traditions range from hatha yoga, often taught to beginners and accessible to seniors, though it also ranges to powerful disciplines along with others such as kundalini and ashtanga.

Yoga is inherited from Ancient Vedic teachings of 7000 years ago, a practice associated with attaining a state of "permanent peace or bliss." Yoga is a Sanskrit word meaning union, interpreted as union with the divine. Later ideas associate it with samadhi or concentration leading to union with the divine, and another to yoke. Someone who practices yoga or follows the yogic philosophy with a high level of commitment, is called a Masculine yogi or Feminine yogini. The ultimate goal of Yoga is "liberation."

Incorporating yoga at any age, is fun and of great benefit to creating a flowing connection with Body, Mind and Heart. Attention to Breath and stretching movements bring the focus inward, like a moving meditation. Most classes are set up so one can progress at their own pace. Attending classes until developing our own routine is an optimum way to learn and integrate this Ancient Art into the Life. *For those so drawn, yoga is a wonderful addition to the self-healing awakening journey!!!*

Naturopathy

Naturopathy, or naturopathic medicine, is a form of alternative medicine supporting vital energy or vital force of the bodily processes such as metabolism, reproduction, growth, and adaptation. Naturopathy favors a holistic approach with non-invasive treatment and generally avoids the use of surgery and drugs. Among naturopaths, there is a broad range of treatment and support for wellness.

NAET

This is another brilliant, gentle effective method to rewire the neurobiology, from which we have seen profound results. NAET uses a gentle systematized approach to remove sensitivities, pain, allergies, vaccination residual, through a combination of meridian stimulation and homeopathic doses of allergens.

> According to Oriental medical principles, "when the body is in perfect balance, no disease is possible." Any disturbance in the homeostasis can cause disease. Any allergen capable of producing a weakening muscular effect in the body can cause disturbance in homeostasis. Hence, diseases can be prevented and cured by maintaining homeostasis. According to acupuncture theory, acupuncture and/or Acupressure...is capable of bringing the body to...homeostasis by removing...blockages from energy pathways known as meridians. When the blockages are removed, energy can flow freely through the energy meridians, bringing the body in perfect balance.
>
> *NAET, naet.com*

"NAET® was discovered by Dr. Devi S. Nambudripad in 1983. Nambudripad's Allergy Elimination Techniques, also known as NAET, are a non-invasive, drug free, natural solution to alleviate allergies of all types and intensities, using a blend of selective energy balancing, testing and treatments...from acupuncture/acupressure, allopathy, chiropractic, nutrition, kinesiology.." Over 12,000 practitioners Worldwide. www. naet.com This type of "rewiring" is very helpful for the ***21st Century Superhuman, Quantum Lifestyle*** toolbox for clearing and creating balance, so that we can continue unwinding our self-healing journey gently and with ease.

Chiropractic

Chiropractic is a familiar methodology, yet a broad range of practices are embraced by many chiropractors supporting wellness. Thought of as regarding the spine, yet broadly it is about balancing energy channels of the body. There are many excellent chiropractors and a broad range of methodologies. When seeking a practitioner, find one whose work is particularly effective for *you*.

CRA - Contact Reflex Analysis

CRA®, a focused type of "muscle testing" scores the body's reflexes to determine what the body needs to operate at the greatest vitality in all situations. It is practiced by chiropractors and other practitioners trained in it, can be found by searching online. It is an excellent, non-invasive system using the body's bioelectricity to determine how to achieve optimal function.

Contact Reflex Analysis was developed by Dr. Dick Versendaal, D.C. with whom Teddi had the good fortune of interning and sharing clients with for over twenty years. Dr. Versendaal said, "It's about connecting the Brain and the Heart which is where the Soul resides;" and quoted DD Palmer, founder of chiropractic, "Too much or too little energy is disease." Several of his books are available online with details.

When you're right with Innate, Innate is right with you.

D.A. Versendaal D.C.
Founder, Contact Reflex Analysis

Dr. Versendaal describes how CRA® works, "Research has proven the human body to be like a computer, made of the brain (electrical generator and memory bank) and thousands of miles of...nerves, connecting every organ, gland and tissue of the body. They also connect with "breaker switches" called contact reflexes. By contacting these reflexes, using the body's muscular system as an indicator, we are able to monitor function of body systems." *Standard Process* products often used with CRA®.

Homeopathy

Homeopathy began with the work of Dr. Samuel Hahnemann (1755-1843) who as a physician was disillusioned with medical treatment of the day. He developed a system of taking energetic doses of substances to remove the same symptoms they caused in physical doses. He developed the philosophy, "Let like be cured by like."

A homeopathic remedy is made by diluting the substance into potencies shaken in water hundreds of times until there is no physical substance left, only the energetic frequency of the substance that Creates the symptoms. When ingested or even sniffed by the "patient" it can negate symptoms and participant moves toward wellness.

Homeopathy is noninvasive, can provide amazing results, yet is a bit complex with thousands of remedies. Homeopaths take a case history to determine a remedy to help restore vital force, assisting the body to move into its own healing process.

HOMEOPATHIC FIRST AID KIT: A homeopathic first aide kit, with low potency remedies 30c can be used in everyday situations with outstanding results. Most come with a small description sheet covering main symptoms of each remedy with with which one can easily work through symptoms that arise of cold, flu, insect bites, wounds and other everyday occurrences. A simple book and first aid kit is a great way to learn and use homeopathy at home. For more in-depth situations it's best to consult a practitioner who is familiar with remedies.

I had a brown recluse bite on my foot and was able to take homeopathic remedies from my first aid kit and work through the symptoms as each new symptom emerged, I would take another remedy for that symptom and within two weeks the bite was gone. ♥ *Cary*

Radionics

Radionics uses a non-traditional form of homeopathy. A small machine measures electromagnetic *Fields* through meridians or energy pathways of the body, providing a readout that can then be fed through a plate or device into water. The water becomes potentized with these energetic frequencies that when taken then assist to neutralize those patterns in the body. Such a process is a gentle powerful support for moving into greater balance. Radionics is supportive of stronger Life-Force for plants, pets and people.

I have known excellent practitioners over the years who use radionics machines. These simply require a photo, hair or some representation of the person, in order to determine correct frequencies to potentize a bottle of water to be a matching energetic signature or imprint, for the symptoms the person, pet or plant has. A traditional homeopath would consider this a transgression, however I have seen profound results with this science also. Radionics machines work with rates and frequencies, and Create a homeopathic response to eliminate the pattern of the dis-order or dis-ease from the body. ♥ *Teddi*

Electromagnetic Frequency Machines

Numerous sophisticated energy machines are leading us into our future of healing, with energy frequencies and waves. Energy healing is Now suggested by the American Cancer Society: "Electromagnetic therapy involves the use of electromagnetic energy to diagnose or treat disease...low-voltage electricity, magnetic *Fields*, radio waves, electromagnetic energy generated for this purpose. Some systems: BioResonance Tumor Therapy, Rife machine, Zapper...and more."

Electromagnetic therapy, lasers, light, electromagnetic resonance biofeedback, and pulsed electromagnetic *Fields* are available, some developed by NASA and Russian space programs, now found in private sector around the World.

Two types systems exist: Some test the body's meridians for weakness or blockages, returning a homeopathic signal to neutralize or equalize the energy patterns. Others emit frequencies, light or wave patterns, also effective. *What we come back to is this:* use all these wonderful tools to assist the body back on track; *AND* there is only one *"cure all:"* clean cells and oxygen respiration; restoring alkalinity with baking soda, simple natural foods and cleansing of Body-Mind.

One of the greatest scientists in history much of whose work around healing and free energy was destroyed was Nicola Tesla. His brilliant inventions of radio, remote control, alternating current, induction motors and more paved the way for modern society. Royal Rife (1888-1971) developed the Rife healing technology, with the ability to cure cancer, suppressed by the establishment. Rife machines are available today, and emit frequencies to negate cancer, herpes and other disorders. There is a resurgence of healing tools with Teslas' energy discoveries.

> The day Science begins to study nonphysical phenomena, it will make more progress in one decade than in all previous centuries of its existence.
>
> Nikola Tesla (1856-1943)

Nikola Tesla and Royal Rife's work are closely related in the field of Bioelectromagnetic Healing. For a person interested in using these devices further research is suggested to discover possibilities available in this field.

Many astounding inventions have been suppressed by "powers that be" during the last few centuries, (Now diminishing in power as we shift into Heart frequencies where they can no longer exist). As we Live in Joy as free sovereign creative beings, we change our global culture, based in our own true value and well-being for all. Old paradigm systems will no longer hold frequency in our World, as we *shift our resonance* from blame-fear-hostility to embrace our True Design LOVE.

Ralph Ring Natural Scientist worked with Otis Carr (Tesla Prodigy) on Alternative Technologies and Teleportation. He was One of three to pilot a Man-Made Spaceship, the OTC-X1. Ralph works on producing advanced technologies based on Tesla's work at BlueStarEnterprise.com, reminding us that Tesla said our greatest scientific developments will come when we understand them in light of Consciousness.

Our quest on the Earth-plane, is to reopen to the totality of the Heart. *Quantum Lifestyle* claims Health and Longevity as our birthright, using advanced science to Create balance, as we free ourselves from old Vibrational content, shifting our "reality" Now. Doing so frees us to choose wiser, more sovereign Lifestyle practices for ourselves and Loved ones, restoring a Truly Healthy Planetary Earth Community, founded in our True Design, LOVE. ♥

Part 4 Body: Section 3
Dis-Ease The Illusion

God implanted in your mind neural structures which will guide you when they are active. If they are active, you who follow these instructions will come into conscious possession of and be able to use this latent guidance system, designed to make available thoughts and actions that will increase your happiness and well-being.

Yeshua (Jesus)
Aramaic translation of TOUVEYHOUN - Begins each Beatitude, dr. michael ryce

What lens are we looking through? Is the glass half empty or half full? Are you on the way *up* the spiral, or you are you on the way down? A young friend once said "if we're on the Titanic, and it's going down, we might as well party," which many in World have adopted as their philosophy. Based on Sir Isaac Newton's Mechanical Law of Inertia, we know it takes effort to get moving new directions beyond the status quo surrounding us. Let's Be inspired to get our inertia going, as it is so worth it!

Health, Well-Being, Vitality and reversal of dis-ease begin in Mind-Heart. Dis-ease is a *learning tool,* Mirroring to us where we are disconnected from Source - our True Power Supply, where there's a "logjam in the river," or where we still carry thought Not of LOVE. Tools in Part 2: MIND teach us very specific skills to remove this old content.

Learning through pain and suffering "sandpapers us," removing rough edges. Awakening teaches us, *"I'm not my Mind, I'm not my Body, Immortal Self I Am,"* yet it is a Journey to bring this in to focus. Our commercialized culture lures us with every "cure-all" imaginable, take this or that to lose weight, get rid of symptoms or feel good, promising to solve ALL our problems from the outer. The only way these things will truly change is to address the Vibration *inside* us of old thought-emotional energy, holding them in form.

Once we change our Mind-energy we are more willing to implement Healthy Lifestyle habits, such as natural healthy foods, cleansing and detox, to assist the body to move up in frequency, so that old thought-emotional content will surface and be released. Tools and habits harmonize with the Law of Cause and Effect, powerful when rightly understood.

Dr. Esselstyn, Dr. Barnard and Dr. Campbell all demonstrated over 20-30 years, dramatic reversal of potentially *ALL* degenerative conditions in weeks, with vegan low-fat diet. This is also confirmed by *Electrovibratory Rate of Nourishment of Foods* chart in Nutrition chapter. Adopting vegan-vegetarian Lifestyle may seem like a big step right Now, however bless where you are on the path and your own growth process, and consider these steps for Healing, Well-Being and Longevity. As Sun Bear would say, *"The Highest Gift you can give yourself is to Bless Everything and Live as a Blessing to the World."*

Physical detox and clearing of self-destructive thought and habits land us in support of Vitality and Well-Being. Claiming this birthright is one of the greatest steps we will ever take, toward sovereignty and freeing ourselves from self-serving systems. Rewards are Abundance, LOVE, Intelligence and capability to bring our Gifts into the World.

Burdens from past generations' imprints and our early environment are catalogued in our body structure as "crystals" [Dr. John Whitman Ray] or "carbon based data" [dr. michael ryce.] Body and Mind are intertwined, so clearing must happen both from unconscious thought and Body.

If we are stuck in old patterns and covering them up with Life's "obligations," disconnected from the Heart, it's critical to get moving into clearing, releasing, letting go to restore *Essence.* We've developed the cultural idea that if we just "do what's healthy" we'll be fine, yet removing our unconscious "old corrupt data" *is essential.* "Not of LOVE" thought-emotion expresses through eating and living habits that Create a "logjam in the river," which adds up to toxemia in the Body.

So-called dis-ease is a toxemic crisis. When toxins are eliminated...the sickness passes - automatically health returns. But the dis-ease was not cured; for if the cause is continued, toxins still accumulate, and in due course of time another crisis appears. Unless the cause is discovered and removed, crises will recur until functional derangements will give way to organic dis-ease.

J.H. Tilden MD (1851-1940)
Toxemia Explained: The True Interpretation of The Cause of All Dis-Ease

Develop your own pattern of unique healthy habits, shaped around *your* Body-Mind and personal place on the path. Participating from the standpoint of *knowing ourselves,* we use cleansing, mineralization and whole organic foods, superfoods and thought to raise cellular vitality, to assist "corrupt data" to surface and be cleared with LOVE.

High-Frequency Nutrition with hands-on Energy-Balancing by friend or energy worker, opens energy pathways to move out old thought-emotional content. As we remove "corrupt data," we open energy pathways with **21st Century Superhuman Quantum Lifestyle** Habits, inspired by our Newfound vitality. Then our enthusiastic high-frequency Body-Mind-Heart is truly supported in Vitality and Well-Being, and we are on the *Path,* to Living our full Authenticity from the Heart and *Essence,* also known as En-Light-enment. ♥

Part 4: BODY
Chapter 10
Toxemia The Cause Of Dis-Ease

I shall recognize all dis-ease as the result of my transgressions against health laws and I shall undo it with right eating, less eating, fasting, more exercise and right thinking.

Paramhansa Yogananda (1893-1952)
Founder Self-Realization Fellowship, "Autobiography of a Yogi"

D uring the last century excellent foundational principles were developed for reversing and preventing disease, that still hold true today. They taught how design of our body requires cleansing and Light nutrition to prevent and recover from dis-ease or i-llness.

Every so-called dis-ease is a crisis of Toxemia; which means that toxin has accumulated in the blood above the toleration-point, and the crisis, the so-called dis-ease—is a vicarious elimination. Nature is endeavoring to rid the body of toxins. Any treatment that obstructs this effort at elimination baffles nature in her effort at self-curing.

J.H. Tilden MD (1851-1940)
Toxemia Explained: The True Interpretation of The Cause of All Dis-Ease

These valuable principles were described by JH Tilden MD, in his 1926 book, *Toxemia Explained: The True Interpretation of The Cause of All Dis-Ease*, a classic worth reading, available free online. Tilden's foundational principles were adopted by the Natural Hygiene Society and widely used with great success. Retreat centers grew up around these principles of fasting, cleansing, raw and foods and juices, similar to European sanitariums where Tilden gained his early ideas.

To do nothing is also a good remedy.

Hippocrates
Father of Modern Medicine

Foundational principle taught by Tilden is that the Body must be restored to run as a "clean machine." Our cells, bloodstream, organs and glands take in nourishment and eliminate waste. When the system gets overloaded with waste products at cellular, blood and organ level faster than it can eliminate them, "acute" conditions arise, such as stress, exhaustion, cold, flu and fever, as attempts of the body to cleanse and restore balance. Understanding this one principle and how to implement it is *the* Key.

The old saying commonly misinterpreted *"starve a cold, feed a fever,"* actually evolved from this Tilden philosophy, which stated correctly says, *"starve a cold LEST you feed a fever."* This means that ALL illness is the body requesting us to reduce food consumption and support it in cleansing through fasting, juices, living foods and light nutrition. This is what we call a "Healing Crisis." The body is requesting lightening foods, increased fluids, *and* clearing of all Not of LOVE thought (conscious-unconscious).

When confronted with illness, it is helpful to learn to say, "I am cleansing," or "I'm in a detox," rather than saying, "I am sick" (because otherwise this is what we're creating). Follow-up with physical-mental cleansing and detox of Body-Mind. Clearing the unconscious with *Freedom Tools* [Part 2: MIND] addresses how we got "overloaded" or "toxic" in the first place. Then support with Cleansing and Detox, juices, fasting, Ideal Nutrition and Superfoods, with nurturing from natural practitioners, friends and self-care.

Tilden's principles, still true today, are foundational to restoring well-being.

Every so called dis-ease is a crisis of Toxemia; meaning toxins have accumulated in the blood beyond a toleration-point, and the crisis, the so-called dis-ease - call it cold, flu, pneumonia, headache, or typhoid fever - is a vicarious elimination. Nature is endeavoring to rid the body of toxin. Any treatment obstructing this effort baffles nature in her effort at self-curing.

J.H. Tilden MD (1851-1940)
Toxemia Explained: The True Interpretation of The Cause of All Dis-Ease

Repeated overloading the system accumulates toxins and initiates chronic conditions. Cumulative "toxemia" causes suppression of Life-force throughout the Body, resulting in degenerative conditions such as cancer, heart and cardiovascular dis-ease, arthritis, diabetes and numerous other dis-orders. The moment we make different choices with Cleansing and Detoxing Body-Mind, Regeneration kicks in!

Remember, we are *Energy Beings*. Becoming involved in taking care of our own Living vehicle is one of the most exciting, productive actions we ever take, and has been a basic aspect of "waking up," in ALL true spiritual traditions throughout history. We either bemoan our miseries, or engage as Master or Mistress of our Destiny. The *moment* we let go of suppressive habits and clarify thought, nutrition, action and focus, our Life process shifts to move in a *positive direction*. Breathe and Smile.

Taking Health into our own hands by living Response-Ably is one of the most Freeing and self-empowering things we do. It requires awakening from the slumber of television,

108

advertising and general brainwashing common in today's World. Creating alliances with Healthcare practitioners, Naturally and traditionally aligned with us can be helpful.

A physician, naturopath or holistic practitioner can assist with gradually withdrawing from drugs. Natural supplements can assist with this transition, turning suppression into support of Life-force. Modern medicine may "save a Life" to give us "another chance," then practitioners can help restore connection to Life Flow. Interview practitioners to find those harmonious with your philosophy. Find a massage therapist, energy worker, acupuncturist, electro-Vibrational practitioner, chiropractor or medical practitioner comfortable for you, who supports you in Your Journey. LOVE yourself.

True interpretation of cause of dis-ease, and how to cure is an obvious sequence; an antidote to fear, frenzy and the popular mad chasing after so-called cures.

J.H. Tilden MD (1851-1940)
Toxemia Explained: The True Interpretation of The Cause of All Dis-Ease

Pursue your own regenerative process, rather than perpetuating the old "patch it up and get rid of my symptoms" philosophy. Obtain support, nurturing, nourishment and regeneration with well-chosen practitioners, friends and self. **Do your goal canceling process** to remove unconscious thought-emotional content, that Created these blocks in the first place. You may find yourself feeling *TIRED* while in phases of clearing. This is natural as we go through unconscious layers. No matter how deep dark and scary they are, you will never be free until you do your clearing of "old corrupt data." Utilizing numerous resources recommended in this book, we invite you to nourish and cleanse Body-Mind with *LOVE and JOY*. Breathe. Smile. Feeling better is an inside job. Self-LOVE is important.

Every time we align with a "feeling better" thought-emotion, we move in the right direction. We improve, vitality increases, and a sense of well-being takes over as we clear "old data," and take a pro-active role in our self-care. We may hit a "conditional ceiling," where we get to a level of feeling good, yet once there, an old voice inside us says, "I can't do it, or I want to quit." Make this a squeaky or sexy voice just to disempower it! We find the level we're at on the Emotional Tone Scale [Part 3: Spirit] and do more clearing of "old data," [Part 2: MIND] to move beyond tendencies to fall into depressive or suppressed coping. Higher LOVE, extra rest and self-nurturing move us into Enthusiasm! We are here to be Joyful, Creative LOVING Beings. This Journey is about restoring our Authentic Self.

At first to go past a "ceiling" may mean expressing anger or frustration. Share with family and friends you need to do this for your healing, and ask them not to take it personally. Tell them you're having a "clear the shadows moment." Use Goal Canceling to clear items peeking out of your unconscious. Know you may end up doing a "medusa" of worksheets - where one leads into another and you empty the "can of worms," to remove this old thought-emotional toxemia.[Part 2: MIND] Guaranteed, as your Vitality goes up, you *will* access new levels to clear. Be excited as you move past what used to be a "ceiling" and keep moving upscale. This trail leads us to the 6th UNIVERSAL LAW of Cause and Effect, which describes for us how the ever-flowing, Living *Field* of Creation operates:

> Chance is but a name for Law not recognized; there are many planes of causation, but nothing escapes the Law." Every thought-emotion, word and action sets in motion an effect that materializes.

What materializes is a direct result of Vibration within us of LOVE or Not of LOVE *Mind-Energy* [Harvard studies - 5% conscious, 95% unconscious]. Simple. We are not used to thinking about dis-ease and illness this way, so it is a learning process to free ourselves from a system that makes *billions off of our deepest fear and ignorance about laws of Life.* Assist your body with its natural process of clearing thoughts not of LOVE, cleansing, healing nourishment, herbs, oils and connecting with nature's energetic Vibrations. Establish a True Path to Wellness with *self-empowering Commitment to your journey* above ALL else.

This helps us get, Be and stay well. When we Live these secrets, vitality goes up, making it easier to *avoid* what's "going around" and avoid future degenerative conditions by establishing Cleanse and Detox habits of Mind-Body on a daily basis. The secret is *"Keep your house clean!"*...Keep Body-Mind clean. Nourish with cleansing, good food, and energy channels kept open with High Frequency thoughts. *Start today!* Start your day with a quart of warm plain or lemon water to cleanse every day! Simple.

Today's buzzwords for **toxemia** are **inflammation** and **acidity**. *When we are on overload, first comes acidity, then irritation, then inflammation, then fibrins (as seen in Live Blood Analysis) then degenerative illness and death.* Each of these strategies is the body's attempt to cleanse and restore alkalinity. The fibrin stage is the body's attempt to make small fibers to cover up tissues at risk, thus fibrous tumors often precede cancerous conditions. Andrew Weil has written excellent current material on inflammation.

Our nutritional and cleansing programs are ALL designed to alkalize the body, reduce inflammation, and support a clean, healing vibratory condition for all around well-being. Juicing or blending raw vegetable soups, great ways to alkalize the body, have now gone mainstream, with these wonderful methods and how to do them, easily accessible to anyone. Natural programs for reducing inflammation and acidity are popular for a good reason, **they work!** You no longer have to be the "odd person out," or do it on your own. Upscale your Life with friends of common interest and share the journey of renewal.

> We won't beat cancer by any one approach. I believe it must be multifocal. In other words, beef up the immune system, detoxify, eliminate dental infections and toxic dental materials, alkalize your body, oxidize the body with oxidation therapy, and give specific nutrients to throw a monkey wrench into cancer's peculiar metabolic pathways.

Robert J. Rowen, MD
Bitter Melon Article, Second Opinion Newsletter

Toxemia seen through a modern lens, is well handled with regular habits of cleansing and detox, part of an everyday routine. Habits to include for an everyday approach of detoxifying and cleansing include:

- water, tea, fresh juices, fasting
- fresh air, natural environments - earth, air, water, sky, sunlight, moonlight, starlight
- walking, running, swimming, yoga, movement , barefoot
- rest, naps, lucid dreaming, deep sleep, introspection, Breathing
- clear thought, prayer, chanting, gongs, bowls, music, meditation [Part 2: MIND]
- Letting go all old thought-emotion Not of LOVE, clearing-unconscious,
    "goal canceling" [Part 2: MIND]
- I Am Creator: Attention on the *Field* is *always* creating [Part 1: SHIFT OF THE AGES]
- Creativity, flowing, allowing, "going general," releasing to the *Field*
- Joyful Enthusiasm! Laughter, Smiling, Breathing
- Heart Coherence through Deep LOVE, COMPASSION, GRATITUDE
- High-frequency foods and beverages, Superfoods, Water
- Herbs and Extracts, Essential Oils, Homeopathy, Acupuncture, Massage
- Knowing "I Am Creative Being of LOVE," flowing from me to ALL

Doesn't it increase your Energy, just reading this list? When these elements are integrated into the Life, we call it **Quantum Lifestyle!**

Though there are many sincere medical professionals, pharmaceutical companies owned by petroleum companies have hijacked health freedom and knowledge through greed. In hot pursuit of profits their high-dollar lobbying, has instigated laws making it difficult (or illegal) to easily choose the Natural path to Wellness.

Insiders have reported ad campaigns describing dis-ease symptoms 1-3 years prior to release of a drug, so by the time the drug is developed, viewers are convinced they have the symptoms and "must have" the "miracle drug" to "get better." Overuse of prescription drugs is at epidemic proportions, perpetuated by patients *fearfully* desiring instant relief and doctors obliging.

Medical intervention is of benefit, particularly when natural laws of nutrition, cleanse and detox have been ignored. There are many *good* people in medical professions whose greatest interest is well-being of others; yet the system is built around the drug industry's practices of *suppressing symptoms,* rather than encouraging wellness through harmony with Nature. Desire for profit to the detriment of humanity is unsustainable and will not long survive. The more individuals who learn and choose habits supporting Well-Being and we expand our Knowledge and Wisdom, the faster our culture will move beyond this .

If mammograms were really finding deadly cancers sooner (as suggested by the rise in early detection), then cases of advanced cancer should have been reduced in kind. But that didn't happen. In other words, the researchers concluded, mammograms didn't work.

New York Times

Think Progress (online magazine) reports that the megalithic pharmaceutical industry reaped *$84 Billion* in 2012, and *$711 Billion* in the last decade. They continue to shape our medical system into what it is today. NPR's *Talk of the Nation*, Sept. 2011 reported, "Pro Publica investigation shows that many doctors are being paid [to do training, presentation and use equipment] by the same drug companies whose medicines they prescribe." It's easy to take a pill every time we feel bad because our system supports it.

To be well, energized and vital, foundational health requires a clean running body, that establishes its own inner strength. Cleansing and Lightening up nourishment are best resources when sniffles and dis-comforts come around, which also sets us up to avoid later degeneration. This requires self-education and Lifestyle commitment to remove ourselves from the greed-based pharmaceutical system that has dominated our health care industry.

Findings...reveal doctors prescribed antibiotics to 60% of sore throat patients - despite that drugs are only thought to be necessary in about 10% of cases...

Another interesting finding: growing popularity of expensive, broad-spectrum antibiotics such as *Azithromycin,* over tried-and-true drugs like *Penicillin.* Last year the *new York Times* noted that *Azithromycin* "may increase likelihood of sudden death" in adults at risk for heart dis-ease.

Dr. John G. Bartlett, a professor of medicine at Johns Hopkins University School of Medicine, told *the Times* that he believed that overprescription of *Azithromycin* could also contribute to antibiotic resistance. "We use *Azithromycin* for an awful lot of things, and we abuse it terribly," he said. "It's very convenient. Patients LOVE it. 'Give me the *Z-Pak.*' For most of where we use it, the best option is not to give an antibiotic, quite frankly."

If the looming threat of antibiotic resistance isn't reason enough for concern about doctors' free-hand with antibiotics, there's also the considerable cost to our health care system—an estimated $500 million for antibiotics prescribed unnecessarily for sore throat alone between 1997 and 2010. If you include cost of treating side effects of unnecessary antibiotics such as diarrhea and yeast infections, the study's authors estimate costs would increase 40-fold.

Mother Jones
The Scary Truth About Antibiotic Overprescription

Anti-biotic means "against Life." Although there may be times a life is saved by an anti-biotic, they are taken far too often, and kill off healthy microorganisms that belong in the gut. Learning how to Live a healthy *Quantum Lifestyle*, with use of Herbs, Cleansing, Nutrition and Thought fortifies body and immune system, so such drugs are not needed.

One geriatric nurse observing greater confusion and hallucinations with prescribed meds for Alzheimer's said, "Prognosis is the same for patients who take medication and

112

those who don't, the drugs have such terrible side effects I don't know why they are given...." Regular intake of coconut, coconut oil and external use of rosemary oil have been shown to prevent and diminish Alzheimer's and dementia symptoms.

What is average cost for treatment of cancer for one person? $300,000. For the same person to pursue natural treatment to regain wellness, rough estimate is $10,000. Most treatments have been ostracized by the legal-medical system (pushed by big Pharma), to take refuge in less developed countries, and thus difficult to access, yet doable with desire.

What will it take for our "medical" system to be built around cleansing, nutrition and we-llness? Much is up to us. Clear out our blame-fear-hostility from old "corrupt data" stored in our unconscious. LOVE ourselves! Step into self-empowerment. Take Response-Ability for and Live *Quantum Lifestyle* habits to cultivate Wellness. Choose Health practitioners capable of supporting us in this process.

Fidelity oversees 12 million 401K accounts; they reported in 2012 that a retiring person needs $240,000 for out of pocket medical expenses later in Life. Who are they kidding? Shall we wake up to awareness that big business reaps billions from *fear*; *bringing home necessity* to harmonize our Lives with Well-Being through Natural means?

These examples expose how out of balance these systems are, to which most subject themselves. *As there is no 'out there' out there, we have Created this* in Quantum "reality," and we Create change by waking up and changing ourselves. Thanks to the Natural Health movement of the last 50 years many are Now aware. We know fruits and vegetables are good for us, we know Organic is better. Popularity of juicing, cleansing and detoxing has educated many to lighten up. Herbs and essential oils are now familiar and widely used.

We are understanding cause and meaning of dis-ease, and how to take charge of our Health Destiny. Eternal Flow of Life is toward Health and Well-Being, opened with *Quantum Lifestyle* through Nutrition, Thought clearing, Cleansing and Detox. Once eour connection with Natural habits is understood, we are better able to make choices when and if medical intervention can be beneficial or is needed, thus we access Best of both Worlds.

In developed countries 2/3 deaths are from degenerative illness

- one out of five cancer,
- one out of five heart dis-ease
- one out of 6 diabetic related illness.

Is this *"natural?"* Do we even know what *"natural"* is? How far off track from wholesome Natural Life are we? Does this concern us? Modern or SAD (Standard American Diet common in developed countries) is refined, fried, contains fats, sugars, and large amounts of inhumanely raised animal protein, and has been shown to play a pivotal role in this high preponderance of degenerative i-llness.

ALL degenerative and acute conditions reverse when dietary habits are upscaled to whole food, primarily low-fat, vegan-vegetarian nutrition. ALL choices in this direction have been shown to decrease susceptibility to degenerative conditions. Thoughts also play a role in vitality and choice of habits. Old Fear and Hostility are the greatest toxemia, buried in the 95% unconscious, hidden by denial, and root cause of ALL pain and i-llness.

Next time something is "going around," a cold, congestion, cough, sneeze, digestive upset, or just feeling poorly, Cleanse. Drink warm lemon water. Juice. Make sure colon is clean and support with probiotics. Consume Light raw foods, blended soups, fruit and veggies, juices and water. Detoxify and cleanse to support healthy Body ecology. Cleansing clears out mucous in which bacteria and viruses like to grow, activating Healthy immune response. Remove their habitat. Changing Body's ecology in this way increases immune capability and reduces need for anti-biotics! Clear Mind-Heart.

Clearing Ancient pain (generations) assists us to resolve issues at root cause, opening us to greater flow of Life-force. Rather than asking how to "fix me" or get rid of my symptoms with suppressive medication, I clear my thoughts and adopt a Natural progression to healthier Lifestyle Habits. Are you living Authentically or conforming to fit in? Is there a pull between Innate longing to Create and express *Essence*, yet suppressing self to fit into society, causing lowered Life-force resulting in potential for eventual "sickness.?" How many have lived entire lives doing what they're "supposed" to do...dreaming of the real "me" inside, that might express someday? *There is only ONE YOU! That someday is here, Now!* Imagine the possibilities! Breathe and Smile.

> There is a vitality, a life force, an energy, a quickening that is translated through you into action, and because there is only one of you in all of time, this expression is unique. And if you block it, it will never exist through any other medium and it will be lost. The world will not have it.
>
> *Martha Graham (1894-1991)*
> *Influential Modern Dancer, Presidential Medal of Freedom (1976)*

• When we feel good it's easier to be Happy and attain our dreams.

• Vitality, Health of Body-Mind, and habits of Well-Being are products of Thought

• It's easier to feel good when we let go of toxins in Mind and Body.

• How are you doing with adopting high frequency *Quantum Lifestyle* habits?

• *Journey of a thousand miles begins with the first step. And then the next...*

• Our future civilization and even sustainability on Earth, depend upon us reclaiming Ourselves as Creative, Joyful, Beings we are designed to BE!

• *We are Now Waking Up!*

What Vibrational energy is holding resonance in your World? Are there things you can clear? Are there changes you can make in your Lifestyle to be more Vital, Lean, Fit, Healthy, Clear and Radiant in Body and Mind? Contemplate your answers. Activate new "tuning forks" based in LOVE, Heart, *Essence*, Cleansing, Detox, High Frequency Nutrition and *21st Century Superhuman Quantum Lifestyle habits!* Breathe. Smile. LOVE. ♥

Chapter 11

The Curse Causeless
Shall Not Come

(Proverbs 26:2)

When diet is wrong medicine is of no use.
When diet is correct medicine is of no need.

Ayurvedic Proverb

A Course In Miracles tells us anything Not of LOVE is *part of the illusion.*

Nothing real can be threatened.
Nothing unreal exists.
Herein lies the peace of God.

We merge this with our understanding that the *Infinite Field of Possibilities* is an Eternal sea of *LOVE*, constantly creating, surrounding us, bathing and nourishing us, bringing us Life. It can only Mirror our thought as our "reality," for us to determine whether we have thoughts to clear, to align with our True Design. Anything we experience painful or Not of LOVE is showing us what needs to change *in us!*

Illness, sickness, dis-ease, dis-comfort, pain, war, death, loss, suffering, bothersome things in our day, and *even Joy and Happiness* are a product of our own Mind-energy. It is an amazing *Leap* to embrace and absorb. Clearing our thought-content, our "reality" shifts, and Vibration of our New thought is Mirrored around us by the *Field*. This is an endless feedback loop, letting us know whether or not we have cleared everything to LOVE.

One of the first questions that pops up around this is, "What about my 'Loved One or pet or whoever,' is it my *fault* they are sick, died, etc? These things are not "our *fault.*" If we carry a certain Vibrational content in our unconscious, it is simply a law of the Universe that we are will magnetically draw in someone with matching resonance in their genetic or thought history, stored in the unconscious. It is the "hope of the soul" or the nature of the

Field, that we will go through a process or event with this other Being that plays out this resonance, so both have opportunity to become aware of these issues and clear them with LOVE. It is simple, yet can take a bit of getting used to, as this is the Quantum view of Life.

How much *"blame-fear-hostility-judgment-control"* is in us? Are we ready to let it go? Our genetic, experiential and historical memories, with coded thought-forms (conscious-unconscious), tend to run our Lives from the unconscious. We are Now shedding this dis-integrative energy Forever, for self and future generations. Are you ready to Live as a Joyful Being of LOVE, shifting inside so much that all you experience in the world is LOVE for all things, situations and people? Breathe. Smile. LOVE Yourself.

> Millions of people live a one-sided Life and pass on in incompleteness. God has given each of us a Soul, a mind, and a body, which we should try to develop uniformly. If you have led a Life dominated by worldly influences, do not let the world impose its delusions on you any longer. Control your own Life henceforth; become the ruler of your own mental kingdom. Fears, worries, discontent, and unhappiness all result from a Life uncontrolled by wisdom.
>
> *Paramhansa Yogananda (1893-1952)*
> *Founder Self-Realization Fellowship, "Autobiography of a Yogi"*

Do you get a dose of traditional News on tel-lie-vision? How do you feel about severe weather patterns, bombing, war, nuclear plants at risk? Do you wonder what is happening to your food supply, air and water? How do you feel when a terrorist attack, random shooting or sexual affront is broadcast on the News? Dwelling in fear holds such fearful things in form, as our Attention on the *Field*. [Part 1: SHIFT OF THE AGES] Are you ready to reframe and release this *Creation from within YOU so New can form in LOVE?*

You are most likely in a wonderful place, with a wonderful friends, family, relatively comfortable by global standards; yet *what is buried in your unconscious resonating subtly "Not of LOVE,"* (worries, dis-comforts, news)? **What is your most productive self-inquiry, that will allow you to shift awareness to change your "reality" and World NOW?**

> The mark of your ignorance is the depth of your belief in injustice and tragedy. What the caterpillar calls the end of the world, the master calls a butterfly.
>
> *Richard Bach*
> *Illusions, The Adventures of a Reluctant Messiah 1977*

Our Health, Well-Being, Relationships, Abundance, Vitality and even Physical World change, as we clear our "old data" and thus clean up our Vibration. Pollution, Chemtrails, GMO's, leaky nuclear power plants, Love and bank accounts, all change the instant we cancel, release, let go Ancient corrupt Mind-energy (conscious-unconscious-generational-environmental) and step into our *True Design LOVE.* There is more to our existence than meets the eye or has been commonly given credit for; *play with it and let it work for you...*

Biology is the feedback mechanism
for the universe to learn more about itself.

Nassim Haramein
Transformational Physicist, Founder, The Resonance Project

ALL experienced in Body-Mind: pain, pleasure, well-being, dis-ease, are feedback of our thought resonance. It is a puzzle, unwinding what is at cause. How do we do this? We start with what is closest at hand. Whatever issues are up in Mind-Body are revealed by what *WE FEEL*. This is our point of focus, which we use for doing worksheets, the *Ancient Aramaic Forgiveness* freedom tools, to clear issues surfacing. [Part 2: MIND]

The further we dig down, the more we offload "old data," surfacing in the situation. If you have a child or partner with issues, work on **your own stuff**. *This is the only place you can change it.* **Doing the process reveals the process. Committing to actually doing 3-5 worksheets per day, will teach you more about your own internal content than anything else in this experience!** There is no 'out there' out there (no one else). "Cleanup" happens within. Others Mirror what lies in the shadows of our unconscious. At first this is difficult, yet as we unravel these threads they make more sense, and the Lights go On!

Dissolving false premises we have surrounded ourselves with in this modern culture, we recognize how our thoughts "Not of LOVE," hold dis-harmonious Vibration expressing in our Bodies and our World. We begin to recognize, "The curse causeless does not come." ALL the *Field* or *Divine Matrix* returns to us is based on resonance within us. ALL "Not of LOVE" within us, is part of the illusion in which we've been playing. We learn to see truth of our thought being revealed in interactions between self and others. This removes any need for judgment or control, as we take Response-Ability for our own Mind-energy.

> To extend is a fundamental aspect of God... In the creation, God extended Himself to His creations and imbued them with the same loving Will to Create. You have not only been fully Created, but have also been Created perfect. There is no emptiness in you. Because of your likeness to your Creator you are creative. No child of God can lose this ability because it is inherent in what he is, but he can use it inappropriately by projecting. The inappropriate use of extension, or projection, occurs when you believe that some emptiness or lack exists in you [or another], and that you can fill it with your own ideas instead of truth. [LOVE]

A Course In Miracles
Chapter 2 T T-2.I.1., 1-10

A Course In Miracles tells us that we are "creators," that thought projections Not of LOVE are inappropriate projecting. When aligned with Source, we Live in a state in which nothing is needed and ALL is continually supplied. The moment we stop believing illusionary projections, they perfectly disappear, replaced by our restored Vibration in the *Field* of LOVE and its continual supply of LOVE, Abundance, Health, Success and Relationships flowing to us from Source.

> You do not have to continue to believe what is not true unless you choose to...All that can literally disappear in the twinkling of an eye because it is merely a

misperception. What is seen in dreams seems to be very real...The world has not yet experienced any comprehensive reawakening or rebirth. Such a rebirth is impossible as long as you continue to project or mis-Create. It still remains within you however, to extend as God extended His Spirit to you. In reality this is your only choice, because your free will was given you for your joy in creating the perfect.

A Course In Miracles
Chapter 2 T-2.I.3., 1-10

Most on the path of Healthy Lifestyle are aware of good nutrition. We cleanse, detox, go organic, get outdoors, clear Mind-Heart-Body, enjoy movement and implement natural remedial measures when needed. We recognize that *our unconscious "old data,"* is Mirrored in *our "reality,"* by our Attention or "projection" on the *Field*. As we clear "old data" thought-emotion, and purify our vehicle, we return to our resonance of LOVE.

> It's far more important to know what person
> the dis-ease has than what dis-ease the person has.

Hippocrates

Health and Well-Being are based on higher Mind-Energy, from which productive Life flows. When we feel LOVE and contentment, the body releases "LOVE" hormones that make us feel good, such as oxytocin, dopamine, serotonin and opiates. These make us "feel good" and they bring Healthy balance to Body systems, support vital immune response and develop **21st Century Superhuman** state of Heart Coherence! Sadness, anger, fear, worry and negative emotions produce stress hormones, adrenaline and cortisol, weaken immune system, elevate blood pressure and Heart-rate, make platelets sticky, disrupt the body and take us out of Heart Coherence.

> Cellular resonance: it's like when you pluck one string in on two different guitars in the same room - one will resonate with the other, both striking the same note. This Creates a force of attraction, so the peptides resonate with their receptors and come together to strike the emotional chord as they bind.

Dr. Candace Pert
Discovered Opiate Receptors; "Your Body Is Your Unconscious Mind" Audio

Studies reveal that thinking a thought produces a neuropeptide, which travels through the Body to land on a cell activating matching energy. This thought chemistry bathes us internally, so if we're carrying fear or anger inside, we live with the chemistry of fear or anger. If we're attuned clearly to LOVE, Compassion, Gratitude, we are bathed internally with those "chemicals." We are powerfully affected by whatever thought-emotional energy is carried in the unconscious. *Laughter brings more well-being to our Lives than anything.*

Flow of Life pushes us to move beyond self-limiting energies of anger, fear, guilt, self-doubt or sadness. Pain is our awakener. Like bumping a splinter we draw the *perfect person, event or situation* into our "reality," to "Mirror" our own inharmonious Mind-energy. This offers opportunity to clear, cancel, get rid of, release, let go the old thought buried in the dungeon of our unconscious from genetics and early imprints. It requires strong self discipline to actually do the work to remove our unconscious content in every situation. This is the New "aikido" or "dance" of Life. [Part 2: MIND]

Ouch! Our old response might have been to point a finger at "them" and say, "They are to 'blame,' it's their fault." *Now we know better.* Realizing how essential it is to clear these energies from *our* Being, establishes a new Response-Ability pattern. When the situation arises again with a different person or situation, our Life force offers us "pain," asking us to recognize and clear our own blocked energy, to move toward greater clarity and energy. As we utilize tools in Part 2: MIND and Part 1: SHIFT OF THE AGES, we become proficient at this process, and we shift so much internally we discover we have entered an entirely New perspective of Living.

Even choices to use medications, drugs, vaccinations, alcohol, heavy foods and other suppressive substances come from cover-up or denial of inner fear, driving us to conform to societal norms without heeding the voice of our own Wisdom, Heart and Inner Spirit. It takes amazing courage and commitment to address this inner conflict and unwind it. This is why Sun Bear said, *"Only when we LOVE someone or something enough, do we get the lesson."* So pain comes as our great teacher, directing us into clearing to LOVE.

It is our deep LOVE that drives us beyond our ancient fears. It is our deep LOVE that heals us and our Loved ones. Embracing Deep LOVE, Compassion and Gratitude in all situations helps us to choose higher frequency actions. Integrating work and family with Lives based in *Essence* and connection with Heart, our body produces "happy chemicals" making us and all around us Healthier and Happier. Thus we access our True Gifts.

Consider moving beyond a meaningless job. Groom a path for yourself to make changes in a Healthy way. Seek out others ready to share a home, either blood-family or community. By doing so you assist one another to access more LOVE. Discover a way to support yourself that brings Joy to your life. Break out of traditional molds to cultivate this in your Life, restore Health and Vitality to Mind-Body-Spirit. Give thanks. [Part 3: SPIRIT]

★ *Choose Others to Be with who are choosing to learn and practice these qualities...*
  • *What does Unconditional LOVE look, feel, sound like?*
  • *How do we Live True Peace and Harmony?*
★ *The Path of En-Light-enment is Truly A Lifestyle - choose to be with others who:*
  • *Practice the Art of Heart-Centered Living, Meditation and Mindful Speaking*
  • *Be around Others who practice the Art of Living Consciously & Breathing*
★ *Discover Others who Mirror Ways of Living Consciously*
  • *We are ALL Aspects of God Consciousness...*
  • *Choose those who demonstrate Oneness rather than separation...*
★ *Enjoy Alone-Time & Together-Time*

> • *Seek those who understand the flow of Life and are willing to Flow with You*

Teddi ♥

Our current Acceleration or Ascension activated by where we are in the Cosmos [Part 1: SHIFT OF THE AGES] takes us into Awareness or En-Light-enment (to transmit more Light), waking up from the "dream" of our projections, knowing our Immutable Presence is ONE with ALL THAT IS. Here are "two realities" in Quantum terms:

(1)   The zero Point *Field of Possibilities* or *The Divine Matrix* is continually emerging Creation, ever flowing anew from Source.

(2) We are intrinsically One with this *Field*, with All That Is, *"I Am not just the drop within the ocean, but the ocean within the drop." Sufi.* Torus field within Torus field, connects us through our Heart with LOVE.

(3) The *second* "reality" is Illusion, or duality we have chosen to "play" in to rediscover our Oneness. It is our Not of LOVE Mind-Energy, Mirrored from the *Field*, appearing as our "reality." This "reality" is a dream world. The "dream world" of Illusion outside of LOVE, is only escaped by releasing, letting go, clearing, canceling all "old data" Not of LOVE hidden within the unconscious, to restore our True Resonance LOVE. [Part 2: MIND] *True Aramaic Forgiveness*

(4) As we do this inner personal work, we restore connection with our Heart and begin Living from *Essence.* Authenticity is the New En-Light-enment.

An infinitely important concept we are integrating, is that of *two* "Worlds" or levels of "reality;" one is Immutable, Eternal, an ever flowing sea of LOVE, of which our individualized consciousness and Being is an intrinsic part and continually emerging.

The second is like an overlay over the first; our *projections,* our experiments in playing in and focusing around *Not of LOVE* Mind-Energy, exploring duality outside of Oneness. We choose between these two parallel Worlds with self-awareness and reflection; within us is always choice, whether to nourish thoughts of unlimited Health, Abundance and Well-Being or participate in the worry and illusion of dis-comfort, pain, blame and illness.

Anything we experience Not of LOVE is of the Illusion. *Period. Beneath it is the Perfect Blueprint of Pure LOVE, Immortal, Eternal, Ever Flowing with opportunity of continual Creation; into which we reintegrate fully, at ANY MOMENT we choose.*

A Course in Miracles describes these two realities this way:

(1) Knowledge is truth, under one law, the law of LOVE or God. Truth is unalterable, eternal and unambiguous. It can be unrecognized, but it cannot be changed. It applies to everything that [All ONE] God Created, and only what He Created is real. It is beyond learning because it is beyond time and process. It has no opposite; no beginning and no end. It merely is.

(2) The world of perception, on the other hand, is the world of time, of change, of beginnings and endings. It is based on interpretation, not on facts. It is the world of

birth and death, founded on the belief in scarcity, loss, separation and death. It is learned rather than given, selective in its perceptual emphases, unstable in its functioning, and inaccurate in its interpretations.

How this *Field of LOVE* operates with Truth immutable and unchangeable, is the teaching of *Universal Laws*.[Part 2: MIND] Awakening to a new Experience of Life, we discover Creation based in pure LOVE is True and Real. Beyond it is the World of perceptions populated by Not of LOVE, called Illusion - which dissolves the instant we shift into LOVE.

Pain is a sign illusion reigns in place of truth.

A Course In Miracles

We are asking ourselves to bite off a big piece here. To see ourselves and our World in completely New ways than we have for thousands of years. Excitingly Quantum physics scientifically grounds this New perception of "reality" in a very practical way, which spiritual traditions throughout the ages have attempted to transmit. *TODAY* we have capacity to take this all in, even if it *STRETCHES US!* Be patient with yourself and others opening to these new ideas. Let them settle in and take root. Remember there is no time, there is no pressure. *Be LOVE. Smile. Breathe. Grow into this at your own pace.*

Our "reality filter" is the lens through which we view our World. Many learned to view the World through negative filters, associated with Not of LOVE perceptions within the illusion. This negative thought process ties into timelines (marking movement of consciousness). [Part 2: MIND] When we dwell upon this Mind-Energy long enough it becomes our "reality."

This is how "viruses" *begin, in the mind.* We think of a virus as a live thing outside ourselves, yet a virus is a perpetuated negative thought-form, beginning with our choice of how we use our Mind-Energy. Clearing negative thoughts, removes Vibrational frequency in which a virus can live. Even children benefit from gentle support in removing old and genetic thought-forms, to enter more fully into LOVE and keep thought viruses away.

Negative filters are most always the byproduct of a thought virus. Thought viruses are thoughtforms that seek to enslave us [our choice]. When we look through a negative lens, we believe we are victims, that others have negative opinions of us and that we have limited capabilities. A negative filter will in time transfer you to the timeline where the negative reality is manifested.

We are just as able to choose positive filters that empower us and help us live our highest visions, seen in our sleeping and waking dreams. Whereas a negative filter is centered on what you don't want, a positive filter focuses your energy and attention on what you do want. In creating a positive filter, look at your strengths, talents, potentials and desires and forge a new lens of perception that allows you to strengthen your talents, abilities and cultivate new experiences that you desire.

Regardless of what lens or belief you hold about reality, you will find validation in the outer world... Often people are indoctrinated into negative filters as children. After a negative lens is implanted, thought viruses keep people from developing the emotional freedom and spiritual awareness to allow them to see through the viruses's fear loop.

When you begin to live life as you see it through your positive lenses, your mind and Soul become harmonized. From this place of inner peace, you naturally make decisions and choices that help you realize your highest visions and find your place in the new timeline.

Wes Annac, Aquarius Paradigm
DL Zeta: Upgrading our Lens of Perception Shifts us to Fifth-Dimensional Timelines

Becoming aware we are continually creating "reality," we *release focus* from a negative lens, shifting into positive, powerful Creation of LOVE, becoming unstoppable and radiant. We are *transforming* an entire cultural paradigm as **21st Century Superhumans**, by activating DNA codons, with prime focus on our Authenticity, Living in LOVE.

Information is the resolution of uncertainty.

Deepak Chopra MD
Natural Physician, New Thought Author

LOVE is the One Law superseding all laws. LOVE is the energy behind all Creation. We activate continual *REGENERATION* when we center Life in LOVE. Thus the amazing and beautiful becomes the everyday "norm," in our **21st Century Superhuman** Journey.

We Now express LOVE thought-emotion within and through the Vibrational resonance of our Lives. We affirm and call in: *Deep LOVE, COMPASSION, GRATITUDE, Breathing, Smiling, Laughter, Vitality, Well-Being, Health, Joyous Relationship, Living from the Heart, Loving Friendship and Companionship, Expressing from Essence Pure Self-Expression, Service to others, walking Gently on Earth Mother Gaia or Pachamama, Veganism-Vegetarianism, Breatharianism, Dreaming Peacefully, Naturally Flowing Abundance, Happy Children, Loving Families, Communities, Pets, Comfort, Food, Water, Sanitation, Shelter and Needs Met for ALL, Organic Gardening, Nurturing Wild Places, Living Harmoniously with the Earth, Mineralized Soil, ALL Creatures Free, Biocompatible Free Energy Planet-wide, Teleportation, Communication Technologies Furthering Global Mind, Education Expanding ALL Human-Huwom Intelligence and Creativity, Knowledge, Information Shared Freely, Ideas and Creativity of the Many Feeding into an ever Escalating Spiral Positive Evolution for Humanity-Huwomity, each person born with Intrinsic Value Beyond Measure, ALL organization emerges out of Movement Toward the Common Good, peaceful Solutions Honoring Sovereignty of ALL with LOVE.* ♥

Part 4: BODY

Chapter 12

Enviro Toxins

The best way to detoxify is to stop putting toxic things into the body and depend upon it's own mechanisms.

Dr. Andrew Weil
Founder, Professor and Director of Arizona Center for Integrative Medicine at U of A

We all have a good idea that in today's World we have relatively high exposure to toxins in our environment. First let us say, this is a product of Mind-Energy. No matter how long you've been an environmentalist, no matter how hard you've been fighting for good, no matter how convinced you are, it's something 'out there' and "the bad guys" are creating this, no matter how "mad" you are at "them," environmental toxins are a product of the thought-emotional toxicity vibrating within us as a Collective creating this "reality." *Wow! Okay, let's reflect on that...ha!*

We've Lived for thousands of years in blame-fear-hostility culture with Mind-Energy resonating from this focus, rather than our True Design LOVE. We are *Observer-Creators*; our *Attention* upon the *Field of Possibilities*, calls our *"reality"* into being personally and in our World! Vibrations of anger, hurt or sadness about what appears to be going on in the World, holds it in form, until we cancel our goals and clear, release, let it go. Simple, just say, "I cancel my goals that the world be a safe place, that there be no war, etc." [Part2: MIND] We powerfully change what appears around us the instant we change the resonance within us. Removing all "corrupt data" from our unconscious "operating system," focusing Mind and Heart in LOVE, everything in our World changes form molecularly to match our resonance.

> Every conscious thought you have, every moment you spend on an idea, is a commitment to be stuck with that idea and with aspects of that level of thinking, for

the rest of your life [until you change it]. Spending just 10 seconds focusing on a topic that does not serve your interests, is to invest your energy along a path that will continue to draw from you and define you.

Kevin Michel
Moving Through Parallel Worlds To Achieve Your Dreams

The 6th Universal Mutable Law of Cause and Effect teaches us balance out such exposures in the physical World, avoiding substances, removing them and using chelating substances to remove them. Hold the creative thought potential, envisioning our *Field* and our existence as operating as a healthy and beautiful environment for all, "mud between the toes." Let's review environmental toxins we are exposed to in the current state of our World, while we are changing our thinking as a collective Now!

It is an unnatural stress to counterbalance when we are exposed to pesticides, herbicides, household and chemical cleaners, synthetic air fresheners, radiation and metals that disturb the immune system, causing irritation, acidity, inflammation and fibrins. As we detoxify and clear Mind and Heart,we are able to transform results of Not of LOVE "realities" in our bodies and in our World. We offer key points toward further research, pro-action and resources to clear or counterbalance such deviations.

DENTAL: SILVER MERCURY, METAL & ROOT CANALS

Great teeth are awesomely wonderful, and as continual regeneration is our birthright, it will be exciting one day, to align with regeneration and perfect teeth! The greatest challenge today is severe demineralization of soils. If possible, live where you can eat produce grown in soil enriched with rock dust or is naturally mineralized. Thought patterns associated with teeth connect with the throat chakra and our ability to speak Truth. Loss of teeth and dental suppression come with generational waves around karmic suppression of individual voice, left from the blame-fear-hostility culture.

We are now in the midst of releasing this old paradigm, healing ourselves by getting the metal out of our mouths, and allowing the body to open up to higher frequencies. Mercury is the metal of the mind. It is also a potent neuro-toxin, and as long as we carry it in our teeth, tends to suppress Mind-Body, sending the mind in endless loops.

Dan Dieska, DDS, a close friend trained in Higher Teachings, shortened his own life in service to remove this toxic substance. A rare dentist, he said, "My mission is to free people from the illusion of thinking that silver-mercury is beneficial; the best thing for health is to remove it," and he probably gave his life in this service, departing at a young age.

Younger generations who have had only white fillings or none, and/or preventive coating in childhood to prevent decay, congratulations! You are of the lucky ones. You also "came in" as a Soul with less "karma" to clear, easily sharing your voice in the World. Those who have had your silver-mercury fillings removed, congratulations!!! This is not an easy process. Sometimes teeth are lost as a result, yet a preferable foundation for vitality and well-being.

1. Mercury is a potent neurotoxin and does not belong in a healthy body
2. Mixes with mouth vapor and saliva; has galvanic reactions with other metals
3. Chewing, mixed with saliva and heat it becomes methyl-mercury (more toxic)
4. In the brain it suppresses clear thought and is a contributor to degenerative neurological disorders such as Alzheimer's, Dementia, MS, Lou Gehrig's
5. Accumulates in brain, thyroid, spine, kidneys, liver, lungs, glands
6. Found to be precursor to cancer and other degenerative illness; as a toxin it causes inflammation in the body, removal of which supports remission
7. Mind and conversation tend to stay in endless loops rather than resolution

CILANTRO NATURAL CHELATOR: A Japanese dentist ran a urine test with each patient after removing silver fillings. He discovered by chance that those who had soup for lunch with cilantro, excreted more mercury in their urine, cultivating awareness of this easy "poor man's" chelation for mercury, freeing mercury from the tissues. Once mercury is pulled into solution with cilantro or cilantro extract, it is best to combine with carrier to remove it such as chlorella and food grade diatomaceous earth. We have noticed many who still have silver fillings tend to dislike cilantro, because it pulls the mercury into solution. It is good *not* to use cilantro until silver fillings are removed; meanwhile chlorella is helpful to carry away residue.

All metals in the mouth gradually slough tiny particles into the body, affecting brain, neurobiology and overall well-being. Root canals can be a source of chronic low grade bacterial discharge. All of this is outside conventional dental practices, however there is a growing field of dentists dedicated to overall well-being through non-toxic dentistry. Educate yourself. If cost is an issue there are now great resources in foreign countries. For longevity of body and mind, removal of metals is a must! Even gold and gold alloys in fillings and crowns have a suppressive effect.

RESTORING NATURAL BALANCE: Use cilantro and cilantro extract to chelate once fillings have been removed; Pesto made with cilantro instead of basil; add cilantro to soups. Chlorella regular ingredient in Green Shakes. Chlorella and food grade diatomaceous earth (PermaGuard brand) absorb and carry away residue.

RESOURCES:

• International Academy of Oral Medicine Toxicology IAOMT iaomt dot org
• Hal Huggins DDS HugginsAppliedHealing dot com
• Books by Sam and Michael Ziff
• Rescued by My Dentist DentistryHealth dot com

FLUORIDE

Fluoride defenders offer the story that when fluoride is added to public water supplies it improves dental well-being. They originally used a widely publicized two-year study from the 1940s that showed Hereford, Texas to have the lowest tooth decay rate among schoolchildren of any city in the US. What is left out of that story, is that Hereford, Texas is a town in Deaf Smith County, where is found the richest mineralized soil anywhere in the US, left from from ancient seabeds. Primary cause for dental issues: *you got it* - demineralization of soil. Want to fix it? Follow Haymaker's advice and remineralize gardens, agricultural land and the Earth with rock dust, before it requires another ice age to put things right. Anyone who deals with organic whole grains knows Deaf Smith County produces highest quality organic grains and beans as a result of its mineralized soil. Thus evolved a story that Hereford had high fluorine levels in their soil, when actually they had a composite of mineralization that resulted in their good dental record.

Blog.Fluoride-Free Austin tells how this whole story got started. In 1941, the year the US entered World War II, the war machine was gearing up, and fluoride, vital byproduct of wartime production of metals and enriched uranium was acquiring an unsavory reputation for its high toxicity; while government and industry-sponsored scientists were frantically looking for ways to rehabilitate it. A "researcher" reported to the research section of the American Dental Association, that fluoride added to water based on dental history of Hereford, TX, might prove to be "one of the most important discoveries in dental history."

It carried on from there, as fluoride is a byproduct of the aluminum and chemical fertilizer industries. Piles of this waste to be gotten rid of are now sold to cities for their water systems and dental hygiene manufacturers. Most tests run on cities with fluoridated water show that teeth of children drinking fluoridated water are no better than those in the cities that don't, and in fact even in cities with fluoridated water decay continues to increase. Harvard's School of Public Health reported studies showed fluoride may decrease cognitive ability in children.

> July 25, 2012 — For years health experts have been unable to agree on whether fluoride in the drinking water may be toxic to the developing human brain. Extremely high levels of fluoride are known to cause neurotoxicity in adults, and negative impacts on memory and learning have been reported in rodent studies, but little is known about the substance's impact on children's neurodevelopment. In a meta-analysis, researchers from Harvard School of Public Health (HSPH) and China Medical University in Shenyang for the first time combined 27 studies and found strong indications that fluoride may adversely affect cognitive development in children. Based on the findings, the authors say that this risk should not be ignored, and that more research on fluoride's impact on the developing brain is warranted.

> *HSPH - Harvard School of Public Health News*
> *Impact of fluoride on neurological development in children*

Fluoride was used in Nazi Concentration camps and the gulags in Siberia to make prisoners docile and controllable. At the end of the war the Allies discovered tons of fluoride piled it in concentration camps. When it's added to city water the entire population is dosed with what is considered a "medication," without consent and one dose for everyone - depending of course on how much water they drink. It is also absorbed through the skin while bathing and showering, absorbed through tissues of mouth when brushing teeth. You don't have to swallow it: cooking with fluoride in water concentrates in food and beverages; it doesn't cook out. Only 50% is excreted by the body, so it is a cumulative toxin leading to many health problems. It is not a nutrient; it damages bones.

Have some fluoride in your toothpaste?

In 1991, the Akron (Ohio) Regional Poison Center reported that "death has been reported following ingestion of 16mg/kg of fluoride. Only 1/10 of an ounce of fluoride can kill a 100 pound adult. According to the Center, "fluoride toothpaste contains up to 1mg/gram of fluoride." Even Proctor and Gamble, the makers of Crest, acknowledge that a family-sized tube "theoretically contains enough fluoride to kill a small child."

FLUORIDE FACTS

1. Fluoride - main ingredient in rat poison.
2. Fluoride - main ingredient in Sarin nerve gas.
3. Fluoride - main ingredient in Prozak, and cancer and HIV meds.
4. Fluoride - destroys brain function, accumulates in pineal, bones organs and causes cancer. (inflammation)
5. Hitler and Stalin used it in concentration camps and gulags as a mass control instrument to make prisoners docile.
6. Guess why fluoride is added to drinking water? What in us accepts this?
7. Over 170 million people, or 67% of the US population drink fluoridated water. 43 of the 50 largest cities in the country are fluoridated.
8. What do you think fluoridated water and antidepressants such as Prozak are all about?
9. Fluoride damages DNA.
10. Is it worth drinking filtered water, filtering shower, moving to the country?

Three types of filters that remove fluoride are reverse osmosis, deionization (ion-exchange resins), and activated alumina. Each removes about 90% of fluoride. "Activated carbon" filters (e.g., Brita & Pur) do not remove fluoride.

Let's clear our unconscious data banks of all thought-emotion that gives up our own Life to a suppressive, oppressive culture. Lies told about these things are told so big industry can control the wealth of the World and drain Life out of its citizens. It takes a valiant effort to wake up and make waves; to walk a different path than lemmings running toward a cliff. Let's wake up and fly!

RESOURCES:

• Fluoride Action Network fluoridealert.org

• *An Inconvenient TOOTH* - fluoride documentary (currently YouTube)

• Shower Filter plus drink reverse osmosis or filtered water

• Move to the country and drink natural well or spring water

• Get large water jugs, fill with reverse osmosis water (grocery store)

• Personal water container. Plastic trash is epidemic (no small bottles).

• *Iodine Protects Against Fluoride Toxicity* article DrSircus.com

CHLORINE

Disinfecting water with chlorine began in the 1800s when there weren't many choices; today there are alternatives much more supportive of LIFE to be used. It's like a little poison daily with a dash of "chlorine bleach," drink filtered or natural water if possible.

Dr. Joseph Price wrote a controversial book in the '60s, *Coronaries/Cholesterol/Chlorine,* showing that coronary heart disease increased in subjects drinking chlorinated water. He later headed up a study demonstrating chickens fed chlorine-free water were healthier than those given chlorinated water, still used today by poultry farmers. Global Healing Center's blog, Natural Health and Organic Living reports in *Chlorine, Cancer and Heart Disease*:

> There is well-founded concern about chlorine. When added to our water, it combines with other natural compounds to form Trihalomethanes (chlorination byproducts), or THMs. These chlorine byproducts trigger the production of free radicals in the body, causing cell damage, and are highly carcinogenic. The Environmental Defense Fund warns that, "Although concentrations of these carcinogens (THMs) are low, it is precisely these low levels that cancer scientists believe are responsible for a majority of human cancers in the United States."

Dr. Robert Carlson, a highly respected University of Minnesota researcher whose work is sponsored by the Federal Environmental Protection Agency, sums it up, "the chlorine problem is similar to that of air pollution" and adds that "chlorine is the greatest crippler and killer of modern times!" It is just simple wisdom to avoid chlorine if you can. There are more healthy ways to Create sanitary water.

> We are quite convinced, based on this study, that there is
> an association between cancer and chlorinated water.
>
> *Medical College Of Wisconsin*

RESOURCES:

• Minimally charcoal filter for tap and shower

- Hydrogen Peroxide - for disinfecting (10 min application kills HIV)
- Move to the country and drink natural well or spring water
- Get large water jugs, fill with reverse osmosis water (grocery store)
- Personal water container. Plastic trash is epidemic (no small bottles).

RADIATION

One day rather than clean power inventions being suppressed by those making billions in the petrochemical industry, we will break free, and use free clean power on Earth. We envision this day coming soon. (mud between the toes!) In one cubic foot of space there is enough energy to run everything on Planet Earth for 100 years!!!

Meanwhile (due to rage and fear in the collective unconscious that is Now leaving...) we still use nuclear plants with leaking radiation and radioactive waste. Japan's Fukushima plant, damaged by 2011 earthquake is leaking contaminated water at 1 million times normal levels, says Japanese News. There is wisdom today in being aware and protecting from radiation. Hiroshima survivors ate miso soup with seaweed daily; which is basically a daily dose of iodine, minerals and enzymes.

A favorite resource, Dr. Sircus of International Medical Veritas Association, offers information on iodine as protective against radiation, mercury and other environmental toxins. This is an essential resource for today, especially as it's a common deficiency. Consumption of seaweeds has been proven historically beneficial, as is red marine algae. High quality liquid iodine is best,used transdermally (applied to the skin - forearm good). Caution some have sensitivities.

Additionally we are now exposed to a great deal of electromagnetic radiation with barely a person without a cell phone, cell phone towers and networks around the World, computers, baby monitors, portable phones and electricity itself. Leaving behind electromagnetic devices and reconnecting with the Earth is the best solution to restore our natural electromagnetic frequencies. New protective devices are being developed such as holographic stickers. Do your research. Be aware. RESOURCES:

- International Medial Veritas Association IMVA dot info
- Dr. Sircus (founder IMVA) articles and great iodine source
- Miso and seaweed proved protective in Hiroshima (iodine, enzymes)
- Radiationnetwork.com
- Article: Iodine Supplementation HealthWyze dot org

VACCINATIONS

Self-education is essential, rather than yielding to a system that does not have well-being of adults, children or pets at heart. Pharmaceutical companies make billions from vaccinations, which weaken the immune system and are aimed at global population reduction. Waking up to the truth, and taking a stand for health and well-being is critical.

We have absorbed the "fix me" mentality, "just give me a shot and I won't have to take Response-Ability for my own habits and how they affect my body." The theory of toxemia is more accurate than the germ theory. Yes germs grow in a toxic organism; *cleaning up the body keeps us well*, and has long-lasting benefits.

Multiply $35, $45, $65, $95 by millions-billions made by pharmaceutical giants; only by keeping people in the dark (ignorant to the ill-effects of vaccines) can vaccination profit-levels be kept high. Records show a list of 30 people in political positions with the federal government who also work for pharmaceutical companies. Proponent of healthy lifestyle Dr. Mercola, offers *Vaccination Statistics* at mercola.com.

> Pro-vaccination is all that is offered in the media, schools, doctor's offices, PHS, and all government publications. This is a biased one-sided view of vaccinations based much on manufacturer's studies and writings.
>
> Extreme pressures placed on parents to signing permission and accept all responsibility for toxic vaccines. Yet, doctors cannot guarantee safety of vaccines.... Many vaccinations fail to achieve intended immunity and many cause horrible complications (including death)... trade-off not worth the risk.
>
> • 1992 - American Journal of Epidemiology...children die 8 times rate of normal within three days of DPT vaccination.
>
> • Center for Disease Control (CDC) - children who received HiB vaccine ... were **5 times more likely** to contract the disease than children who had not.
>
> • new England Journal of Medicine July 1994 - 80% of children under 5, who had whooping cough had been **fully vaccinated.**
>
> • 1977 Dr Jonas Salk (inventor polio vaccine) testified that 87% polio cases in US since 1970 were by-product of polio vaccine.
>
> • Sabin oral polio vaccine (OPV) is **only known cause of polio** in US today.
>
> • February 1981- AMA Journal found 90% obstetricians, 66% pediatricians **refused** to take rubella vaccine.

Mercury in vaccines has been shown to cause excessive free radicals, found to cause autism. However coming to the forefront now, with understanding of inflammation and fibrin development, due to repeated vaccine failure manufactures attempt to make them more potent by adding immune stimulators, adjuvants. With an injection, a vaccination bypasses the body's natural protective systems, mouth, skin, nose, and gut. Vaccination's also bypass protective mechanism of the brain called the blood-brain barrier causing chronic inflammation. By 7-8 children have been given up to 30 vaccines, when their immune systems are just developing and they are overridden by this massive dumping of foreign substances through the blood-brain barrier from which many never recover.

The brain's immune cells move through the nervous system, secreting numerous immune chemicals, pouring out an enormous amount of free radicals to fight the invading organism. The problem is there is no invading organism, the brain has been tricked by the vaccine to believe there is resulting over-reaction of the immune system, inflammation, acidity and fibrin development. This rush of free radicals created by the body to protect itself against the vaccine creates additional pieces of tissue in the body called fibrins. This is what makes up a fibroid tumor; it is excess tissue that the body creates to *protect itself* from invasion of some sort, such as free radicals caused by the vaccine. A state of inflammation or acidity is being artificially created, resulting in asbestos-like fibers floating through the system, visible in dark-field live blood cell analysis.

Mercola article, *Vaccination Dangers Can Kill You or Ruin Your Life,* reports syndromes known to result from vaccines, obviously a product of this assault on the brain, and its fight to protect itself, resulting in fibrin development are Autism, ADD, ADHD, Gulf War Syndrome, More common neurodegenerative diseases, Parkinson's, Alzheimer's, dementia and ALS. Studies at the University of Wisconsin in Madison are now proving repeated rabies and other vaccines for dogs are equally damaging, causing chronic inflammation, potentially highly at cause in the 60-70% rate of dogs dying from cancer. Nov. 2013, 19 year old Utah boy died of flu vaccine.

Mercola's article answers the question, *what about flu vaccines?* "A recent study by World-renowned immunologist Dr. H. Hugh Fudenberg found that adults vaccinated yearly for five years in a row with the flu vaccine had a 10-fold increased risk of developing Alzheimer's. He attributes this to the mercury and aluminum in the vaccine. Interestingly, both of these metals have been shown to activate microglia and *increase excitotoxicity (inflammation=fibrins)* in the brain. Basically what we're doing with vaccines is initiating chronic brain and body degenerative inflammation .

Once this over-reaction begins in the brain, it does not stop, affecting individuals differently; a severe example is autism, with ADD, ADHD and Alzheimer's run a close second, with more pharmaceuticals used to feed the drug industry. On top of all this billions has been spent by the Gates Foundation to develop RFID tracking chips to be used in vaccines. Sunday, March 21, 2010 Senate Healthcare Bill HR3200 requiring implantation of radio chips to transmit health and banking information with Obamacare chip implants.

Teddi tells the story of her little grandson, one of the brightest children she had seen, and after returning from getting a vaccination with his parents lost that sparkle, which took him a long time to regain with remedial measures. What residual Mind-Energy is limiting Life force culturally? Educating with Truth we make better choices, to exit the *statistical path*. It takes courage to step out of the traces, educating ourselves, and holding hands around a circle of Truth; a circle connecting us with Natural Law, rather than coffers of the "power-over" greed driven machine. ***APPLY Ancient Aramaic Forgiveness goal canceling here! LOVE.***

No parent purposely harms their child. No pet owner purposely harms their pet. We do not purposely harm ourselves. However we must *"awaken from our slumber;"* of generations of subjugation to debilitating and dehumanizing systems and habits.

We are Free Beings. We are Free to Choose. Inspiration comes from gathering in community with like-minded individuals, expanding knowledge for well-being, sovereign in our expression of Life. This requires the effort of taking care of ourselves self-responsibly; changing Lifestyle to that of **21st Century Superhumans** who understand Quantum principles, that we are "creators" of our "reality;" and good health is as close as choosing **Quantum Lifestyle** habits of thought Mind-Body-Heart.

In many chilling ways, drug companies promise us a utopian future without pain, without disease and illness, thanks to prescription drugs. But is the cost more than we bargained for?

Ray Williams in Wired for Success
How the Drug Companies Are Controlling Our Lives Part 1, Psychology Today, May 23,2011

Are we ready to wake up? To make choices to protect our brains, our health and our Lives, those of our children's and pets; and learn how to detoxify our Mind-Energy and our Bodies? Reclaiming our greatest possibilities, rather than submitting to a money-hungry pharmaceutical system, that emerged from the Vibration of blame-fear-hostility in our unconscious thought-emotional container takes courage, commitment and education around natural wellness methods. *Let's restore our True Design LOVE, and Live as vital regenerative Beings.* **Arc the Hologram with LOVE!**

RESOURCES:

• long term recovery - alkalize, NAET, EFT (next chapter)
• NIVC.org, MCIR.org, vaclib.org, knowthelies.com, know-vaccines.org
• articles.mercola.com Legal Vaccine Exemptions (more articles)
• healthypets.mercola.com, truth4pets.org, dogs4dogs.com, synbiotics.com

GMOs

One of the most amazing things about Living on Planet Earth is the millions of species of plants, insects, water creatures and animals that grow naturally, in an incredibly rich and beautiful ecosystem. The modern developed World has built up an artificial lifestyle contained in cities and suburbs, that largely cut off this natural flow of life. Pavement, city buildings, suburban neighborhoods, manicured lawns, pesticides and weedkillers of the insulate us from nature, and push her away.

Have you heard of *SELF-SUFFICIENCY?* Do you consider yourself to be so? What would happen if there were no food in the grocery store? Do you and your neighbors have gardens so you could share food with one another? Or are there growers nearby? Will seeds you bought at the hardware store grow plants again next year? Or are they hybrid?

Hybrid means that two plants have been cross pollinated, to bear bigger-better fruit, but the seeds from that plant will not produce the same as the parent plant. This means you have to go back and buy seeds from the big company that manufactured them. *This ensures they stay in business.*

To grow plants that produce food and save seeds, and produce true to the parent plant the following year, you must start with open pollinated or Heirloom (over 50 year old variety) seeds. Many reading this book today, have likely never grown a garden to produce their own food, though certainly some have. And likely, many may not *want* to produce their own food. Bill Mollison, father of Permaculture, described perfect cities and towns in an amoeba shape; where developed areas, ebb and flow with U-shaped areas of farms, gardens and farm markets, *an ideal symbiosis.* We might imagine this is a wonderful way to *re-Create cities and towns.*

Healthiest foods for our bodies are those that have grown and evolved naturally with the Earth, so *it benefits us to maintain open pollinated or Heirloom seeds.* Heirloom or open pollinated seeds are those plants that have evolved by natural selection as the healthiest over time. They produce the *BEST TASTING* and most nourishing vegetables and fruits. Whether we are growing a garden ourselves, or supporting growers in our community, obtain foods a grown from Organic, Heirloom or open pollinated seeds. Cultivating neighborhoods and communities, where this is the type of food produced and shared is an essential type of *Self-Sufficiency* we benefit ourselves by returning to.

When exposed to hybrid or GMO pollen, open pollinated or Heirloom seeds become corrupt, and are unable to pass on their genetic heritage of a pure healthy plant that evolved with Earth Mother Gaia to their offspring. Enter GMOs, which we've figured out are causing health problems.

WHAT ARE GMOs? " Genetically modified organisms" are plants and animals that have been engineered with DNA from bacteria, viruses or other plants and animals, with sophisticated technologies such as retroviruses and gene guns, combining genes from different species that cannot occur in nature. GMOs have the capability of destroying all natural food production, eventually leading to total reduction of food sources. Corporations pushing this "cloning" are unthinking of anything but their own profit. *APPLY Ancient Aramaic Forgiveness goal canceling here!*

Virtually all commercial GMOs are engineered to withstand direct application of herbicide and/or to produce an insecticide. Despite biotech industry promises, none of the GMO traits currently on the market offer increased yield, drought tolerance, enhanced nutrition, or any other consumer benefit. A growing body of evidence connects GMOs with health problems, environmental damage and violation of farmers' and consumers' rights. Bt GMO corn, designed by Monsanto to kill corn borers by perforating its gut, has now been found in the guts of humans, causing sensitivities and new illnesses. Monsanto's global efforts to take over food production with GMO seeds in undeveloped countries are relentless. A friend from the Philippines tells of growers bringing in hybridized rice to plant. Local farmers planted the modern seeds on the front edge of the rice paddies, as they knew inspectors wouldn't walk into the paddy. They planted traditional seeds in the back.

Far beyond hybridization is a no man's land of GMOs, experiment in the unnatural, that cannot bode well for the health and well-being of living things. The problem is it that GMOs do not stay put, they infect nearby *Fields* polluting with Frankenstein-like qualities, incapable of producing young.

A Global leader on open pollinated seeds is Vandana Shiva, E. Indian environmental activist and anti-globalization author who has written over 20 books. Time Magazine identified Dr. Shiva as an *environmental "hero"* in 2003. She has been awarded the *Right Livelihood Award, Sydney Peace Prize* and *Fukuoka Asian Culture Prize;* in good company with Nelson Mandela and the Dalai Lama having been one of the few recipients of the *Gold Medal for Peace with Justice.*

Internationally known for encouraging, teaching and promoting seed saving to eradicate poverty, Create self-sufficiency and independence, she has initiated a national movement to protect the diversity and integrity of living resources, especially native seed, promotion of organic farming and fair trade. *She is in a 3 year project with Bhutan to become the first 100% organic sovereign country.*

GROW YOUR OWN GARDEN WITH HEIRLOOM SEEDS: If you have a yard and can grow a garden, grow your own food with heirloom seeds. The next best thing is to support growers in your neighborhood or area by buying local organic food. Creating a viable future means participating in critical choices about where our food comes from, how it is grown, and what its actual nutritional quality. Sept. 2013 UN report, "Wake Up Before It's Too Late links global security and escalating conflicts with the urgent need to transform agriculture toward what it calls "ecological intensification" with local small gardens.

Remineralized soil, open pollinated heirloom, organic, every little choice makes a big difference. Participate in getting us back on track rather than derailed as a modern culture.

YOUR FOOD CHOICE MAKE A HUGE DIFFERENCE: Growing food in your yard makes a huge stand for the future, with Organic, Heirloom, Open Pollinated, Locally Grown food sources. Teach others the same; Neighborhood gardens, seed exchange.

Holding LOVE, Breathing, Smiling. No GMO. And YES many good things! It is our choice. Make the choice rather than leaving it to chance. Live organically with LOVE on Earth. Change our Vibration - change the World. *Arc the Hologram Now with LOVE!* ♥

- Non-GMO Project nongmoproject.org • Permaculture Magazine • Urban Farm
- Heirloom, Open Pollinated Seeds • LAGuerillaGardening.org
- peakprosperity.com • Baker Creek Heirloom Seeds rareseeds.com

Part 4: BODY
Chapter 13
Miraculous Tales

---

*If we are creating ourselves all the time, then it is never too late
to begin creating the bodies we want instead of the ones
we mistakenly assume we are stuck with.*

Deepak Chopra MD
Natural Physician, New Thought Author

*T*he biggest gift I ever got, was when I was holding points on this man, and he was yelling, "Stop it, stop it, you're hurting me, get your elbow off my backside you @*%^!!! John Ray walked over to me, and looked at me with those big blue eyes and said, "Stop resisting his resistance." It was like a giant light bulb went on in my head!" ♥ Teddi

Most importantly what we learned over may years from Dr. John Ray, dr. michael ryce, Tony Robbins and others was "Go into the pain," "move through it with tools and focus." Any area we are uncomfortable in Life or "suffering" physically, mentally, emotionally, our pain shows us where the "logjam" is in the river of Creative flow from Source, where old thought-emotion blocks our Life from being vibrantly well. Elevating Vibrational rate of nourishment, using remedial measures to strengthen Mind-Body to enter its full regenerative capacity are Vital Keys to generate greater Life-Force.

'Wizards? Do you mean they do things a different way?' 'No, just the way we do,' Merlin replied. With a flick of his finger he lit the soggy heap of kindling that Arthur had gathered... A blaze leapt up on the instant. Merlin then opened his hands and produced food out of thin air."

Deepak Chopra M
The Way of the Wizard: Twenty Spiritual Lessons for Creating the Life You Want

The secret to becoming a "wizard," or bringing forth our natural capability to produce miracles, lies within regular practice of moving beyond any tendency to go into denial with food, drugs, alcohol, rage, busyness, and fine tune our ability to clear conscious-unconscious content Not of LOVE.

We must practice peace, harmony, individuality and firmness of purpose and increasingly develop the knowledge that in essence we are of Divine origin, children of the Creator, and thus have within us, if we will but develop it, as in time we surely must, the power to attain perfection. And this reality must increase within us until it becomes the most outstanding feature of our existence.

We must steadfastly practice peace, imagining our minds as a lake ever to be kept calm, without waves, or even ripples, to disturb its tranquility, and gradually develop this state of peace until no event of life, no circumstance, no other personality is able under any condition to ruffle the surface of that lake or raise within us, any feelings of irritability, depression or doubt.

It will materially help to set apart a short time each day to think quietly of the beauty of peace and the benefits of calmness, and to realize that it is neither by worrying nor hurrying that we accomplish most, but by calm, quiet thought and action become more efficient in all we undertake.

To harmonize our conduct in this life in accordance with the wishes of our own Soul, and to remain in such a state of peace that the trials and disturbances of the world leave us unruffled, is great attainment indeed and brings us that Peace which passeth understanding; and though at first it may seem beyond our dreams, it is in reality, with patience and perseverance, within the reach of us all.

Edward Bach M.D. and F.J. Wheeler M.D.
The Bach Flower Remedies

Lynn McTaggart, British investigative journalist noted in her book the *Field*, that *everyone,* even those who don't think they do, have "paranormal" abilities including telepathy and remote viewing. We barely grasp the full extent of possibility of using these subtler abilities, as for centuries superstition has held us back from these Innate talents. Whether we recognize it or not, we have Infinite access to the miraculous.

Just as one person may be able to wiggle an ear or an eyebrow and another read minds, we each have special skills or "super" abilities if you will. Leaving behind limiting beliefs from "the World is flat" mentality, we open ourselves to access these "paranormal" abilities dormant within us, just waiting for us to practice and add them to our repertoire, as we expand into who we are becoming and what is emerging within us, during this Evolutionary Leap the *Shift of the Ages.* [Part 1: SHIFT OF THE AGES]

CATCH YOUR DREAMS: Routinely note your stream of consciousness. Prime time is on awakening or just after focus, meditation, goal canceling or any awareness practice. Lucid dreaming flashes of genius have been measured at 40 Ghz Gamma brain waves, tapping into our "paranormal" abilities. To capture more awareness in this zone, when you are awake during the day, ask the question, "Am I awake"? When you become aware in lucid dreaming you may be cognitive to ask the same question, and then direct your lucid dream! Record your notes without judgment! Enjoy what comes forth as messages from your super-conscious!

Spontaneous Remission

In 1993 the Institute of Noetic Sciences IONS, founded by Astronaut Ed Mitchell, published *Spontaneous Remission: An Annotated Bibliography* at their website. It is the largest database of spontaneous remissions in the World, containing 3,500 cases from 800 journals in 20 languages. This phenomenon may not be as rare as was once thought, as reported cases have increased in recent decades. Embracing this concept assists us to recognize the continual process toward wellness flowing into our Being. If spontaneous remission is so possible, some may ask, "then why did my Loved One die," addressed in various ways throughout the book.

Spontaneous remission generally reported as a rare occurrence, is actually readily available to us. It is supported by clearing Not of LOVE content from our Being, then accessing Light or ever flowing Source *Field* energy, opening pathways for Higher Frequencies to flow. In spontaneous remission, an individual enters into their *Essence* as Light, connection to God, Source *Field*, continuous Creation or Eternal flow of Being, accessing a state where their Body instantly restructures. Our "Light Body" amplifies when our attention is focused in this way.

Highest, Healthiest Intention is LOVE

Marcel Vogel, was born in San Francisco in 1917. At age six he was pronounced dead from pneumonia, yet within a couple of hours to everyone's surprise, had come back to Life. In his early teens he was so dedicated to serious pursuits, he walked to mass daily and was "told" he would bring forth progressive books and inventions, which he did. He spent 27 years as top scientist for IBM and developed 150 patents, among which was technology that evolved into today's computer hard drives.

Marcel's greatest legacy was that he devised ways to measure energy emanating from thoughts and emotions. He developed the Vogel Cut for crystals, with a 51 degree angle matching the Great Pyramid in Egypt, and researched the *Secret Life of Plants*. His crystal cut is still legendary. He also demonstrated that quartz crystals send out frequencies and amplify thought. [Tree of Life Tech carries on his work today.]

Vogel showed the world scientifically *(those who would listen)*, that a person's highest and healthiest intention is LOVE. He found that...any intention is amplified and transmitted with phenomenal change happening to the energy of that intention. This he clearly showed *(for all who would see)* that this is a little understood yet perfect, and perfectly manifesting Life-giving energy force. ...He found and showed others how to connect to themselves and their higher selves with a simple tool. Therefore connecting through themselves to the energy that makes them.

Tree of Life Tech on Dr. Marcel Vogel (1917-1991)
Energy Scientists and Developer of Vogel Crystals

Recall Generational Memory In Utero

Our powerful thoughts emerge into words and deeds, affecting seven generations, though literally to infinity. Our gene pool is run by and inherits the resonance, programmed by our thoughts-emotions and those of our generations. Clearing thought stored in unconscious Not of LOVE, we clear timelines, offering better "realities" to future generations. This generational story fascinatingly demonstrates how thought is passed on from one generation to the next, a favorite from our Body Electronics point-holding days.

A friend participating with us at Health and the Human Mind with Dr. John Whitman Ray, had a 3 year-old daughter with a fever, sleeping on on a pallet on the floor. Our friend K and her then partner B were gently "holding points" on the little girl as she slept. Suddenly the little girl tossed and turned, muttering in her sleep, "Oh no, not now...Oh no, not now..."

K looked at B aghast! "That is exactly what I said the moment I realized I was pregnant with her!!" This amazing example brought home to us and our classmates, how specifically thoughts, words and emotions are stored in the Body-Mind continuum; passed on for each generation to sort out and re-live, unless brought into consciousness to be cleared!

It is amazing that we can access parents, grandparents and 10,000 generations of thought resonating within us, handed down through family dynamics. Wherever we have resistance (old energy Not of LOVE), thoughts-emotions are Vibrationally stored until removed. If we have *any kind of physical ailment or condition*, handed down to us from our family line, we absolutely *must* clear the Mind-energy related to this, to accomplish wellness. We've heard many stories over the years, too numerous to count, of families playing out unmistakable patterns from former generations or bloodline idiosyncrasies. Think of what your family physical and behavioral patterns are.

Young children, barely old enough to understand, recount stories from in utero and of past generations or past lives, that can be traced back to accurate historical records! The wonder of the "holographic mind" shows through its Vibrational patterns and memories so perfectly how we can both imprint and clear past and future generations by clearing ourselves. Historical resonance of thought-emotion imprints on timespace or the 'No - Time' continuum. As we shed old thought patterns we participate with Greater Awareness in this connected Life-process, changing history with clearing, cleansing and LOVE.

In every deliberation, we must consider the impact
on the seventh generation...

Great Law of the Native American Iroquois Nation

As we clear unconscious Vibrational content from generational dynamics, we open ourselves to greater healing potential. Whether or not we have biological children our entire gene pool shifts as we do our clearing, through timespace like dominoes. Ultimately we all are related, and there is no time or space, for we are One and *we are our own ancestors...* We emerge as the miraculous beings we were designed to be, supporting ALL on this Journey of returning to *Essence*! Breathing, Smiling, Changing ourselves, changing the Whole. *Arcing the Hologram Now with LOVE!*

> We should seek not so much to pray
> but to become prayer.

St. Francis of Assisi (1182-1226)
Order of St. Francis

Activation from Celestial events in our Cosmos immerses us in an entirely New energetic matrix in the Earth-plane, opening us to a New perceptions of Being. Deep adaptation is taking place within each of us, activated to heightened states of Awareness, triggered through exposure to Greater Light in this Evolutionary shift. As we open our Hearts to creative aspects of our *Essence*, we also open to our miraculous healing potential.

Once we learn to LOVE everyone unconditionally, releasing need to judge others and self, learning to use the Light of the Creator, we will be able to manifest everything we need to live in harmony and in the new World. We then become Masters, helping others in their spiritual ascension process.

Cynthia T. Crawford, sculptor
Working with the Star Beings to Awaken Humanity

Miraculous Messages for Healing

Anya Petrovic received a "message" from Sai Baba (1926-2011), "Pranic Energy in the Ionosphere, as you call it, will soon solve the issue of the shortage of energy for humanity. However, for this to take place there must be a total renewal of habits and customs that characterize [humanity] now..." She next received a message, "from a young girl from Serbia who had channelled 'Estella from Constellation *Grui*' since age twelve." Anya tells the amazing story, "She found me on the internet and handed me texts as Estella advised her. I read it, found it very interesting and set it aside. That year she gave me the same text *again*, guided by Estella."

Through these messages Anya was led to the realization, she was to assist with human evolution by using Tesla energy from the *Field* surrounding us, to bring the body into "perfect Light balance." Based on healing insights transmitted to her by Nikola Tesla, Anya calls this reactivation of Light in the body, "Tesla Metamorphosis." Clients report speedy, often miraculous recovery. She is attracting Attention from science, as "incurables" such as HIV, cancer, coma, spinal injuries and deformities resolve. In her work and teaching, hands act as a Tesla coil, activating Light in the Body, triggering DNA to Reconstruct.

She teaches that Consciousness Evolution is essential currently on Earth. "We must advance ourselves to become multidimensional Beings; go beyond the logical mind, open to our extrasensory ability, so we can evolve with Earth and Cosmic changes." She tells us, "there are no such things as miracles; these already exist in nature. *The miracle is what we are willing to open our minds to, accept and understand.*"

> ...the miracle entails a sudden shift from horizontal to vertical perception. ...giver and receiver...emerge farther along in time... The miracle thus has the unique property of abolishing time to the extent that it renders the...time it spans unnecessary...it substitutes for learning that might have taken thousands of years.

A Course In Miracles
Page 8, Chapter 1:2-6

After *Tesla Metamorphosis* sessions clients report seeing people, angels, or landscapes different from planet Earth, feel a physical touch, or similar observations during the session. It seems that those healing frequencies open communication with other dimensions and parallel planes of existence. Throughout the sessions, purple violet Light has been recorded transmitting through Anya and participants. Even one year later participants still have the violet color surrounding them, as is shown in special images. Anya says, "There are significant changes happening in the electro-magnetic field of our planet Earth in this period of time. The consciousness evolution of the human race is of crucial importance and a prerequisite to undergo this transition."

At this key moment in Earth's history Lightworkers are emerging, bringing through healing, restorative energies from other dimensions. We will be led to those by whom we are ignited to Evolve, as a result of being with them. This is where it is important to attune to our own intuition, and follow through when directed.

Thousands of generations of history in the blame-fear-hostility paradigm, is Now like an old shoe we are ready to kick off for the last time. Freeing ourselves from these shadows, we awake to our *Essence*, to bring Greater Unity to Collective Conscious of humanity. Are you stepping into *Essence* to Live from the Heart?

The powerful grid system of Light in the energy matrix of Earth is raising by the many holding LOVE and Light on the Planet today. These new frequencies are influencing thought patterns of everyone on Earth. Its power and influence is growing and expanding as millions Now join in. Each person "waking up" has a natural ability to attune to this network and add to its effectiveness. The more "waking up" add to exponential change.

Life is a transformational journey. The more we open ourselves to possibilities that go beyond what we've always believed in the old paradigm explanation of our World, the more we open ourselves to experiencing the miraculous. We are like little ones just learning to walk. We are being reborn from old ways, developing new skills and a new experience base. It's good to try it out and *laugh at ourselves.* There are always tumbles before little ones take their first steps. And then there are those who just stand up one day and walk! Shifting energies Now activate us, to step into Beyond where we've ever been.

Healing Cary's Broken Arm In 6 Hours

Experience gives confidence to move forward and test it out again and again, until we strengthen our muscles with practice, courage, inspiration and commitment. We were blessed to have miraculous happenings decades ago under tutelage of Dr. John Ray. In fact, before we ever went to class with him, we used his teachings to experience a miracle of a broken arm healing in a matter of six hours!

I (Cary) was co-directing a wheatgrass institute in southern Michigan in 1980-81. A young couple came from Bloomington, Indiana, handed me 6 audio cassettes, and told me I must listen to them! Little did I know at the time what "angels" they were! I never saw them again, so I hope if they read this they will contact me. Of course, curious, I listened to the tapes. Somewhere right around that time Teddi visited the Institute, then called Hippocrates, (later changed to Creative Health) where we met for the first time.

During this visit Teddi and her then husband Lou connected with me, and we became fast friends, "Soul family," who had already known each other for aeons... so of course, I shared the tapes with them. On suggestion from these amazing tapes by Dr. John Whitman Ray, we ordered a case of strange-tasting liquid minerals "to get our electrical potential up." We tasted them, and immediately said, "ugh!" there is no way we'll drink that "nasty tasting stuff," (so they sat in a corner at Teddi and Lou's farm).

Shortly thereafter I met Bill who I would eventually be married to for 12 years, and had much of my own "issues" begin to surface from past relationships, and as a "result" fell ice skating, breaking my arm. One friend encouraged me to go to the hospital, based on the suggestion that if we wanted to fix it, we needed to know if it was broken. Sure enough, X-rays showed 2 fractures in upper and lower arm; doctors wanted to immediately do surgery and put two pins in. My arm was in a sling, and as I looked at the x-rays I made a life-changing decision, to leave the hospital and use Body Electronics to fix it. I signed multiple release forms to get out of the hospital and went home. I talked to my group of friends, and convinced them we should heal my arm with Body Electronics.

The next day Teddi, Lou, Bill, Jamie (co-director of the wheatgrass institute) and his then wife agreed to "hold points" on me. We called one of Dr. Ray's students, Robert Stevens, who was practicing in a city an hour away. He explained the methodology to us: hold STO points at base of skull, glandular reflex points on feet, and hold points as close to the break as possible, on the opposite side of the break from the heart. We chugged down minerals (that had been sitting in the corner), I lay on a massage table, everyone positioned around me to hold points.

Lou was at the base of my skull, and every time I'd process a thought into consciousness, by "going into the pain" and releasing unconscious content connected with it, his fingers would burn and he'd give me feedback, "Whatever you're doing, keep doing it." This was a several hour process through which my friends kept their fingers faithfully glued to points that were now giving off searing-burning heat. I kept going into the pain, allowing emotions connected with the pain to rise to conscious awareness, till each emotion moved up the Emotional Tone Scale to LOVE, transmuting them all one by one.

After a couple of hours of fingers faithfully 'mashed" into points, through numbing, burning layers, something amazing happened...suddenly a searing burning heat began to go through my arm, Jamie's fingers followed it up along the break, as the intensity increased and increased. We could literally hear bones click back into place, black and blue patches cleared, muscles that had been hanging and out of place moved back to where they belonged, and as if it had never been broken, my arm was restored! The searing burning current going through my arm dissolved and it was whole! We held points on it for a little while the next day with additional help from friend Len, for residual cleanup while riding in a van on the way to Manitowish Waters, Wisconsin, to go to class with Dr. John Ray. Tiny pieces of bone clicked back into place, and my arm has been fine ever since! ♥ Cary

This amazing experience of a broken arm healing in a matter of hours, reflected several things. There was a great deal of True Connection with Source happening in Hearts and Minds of those in our group. Most were deeply committed to individual spiritual paths, meditation, high frequency nutrition, with faith and vision that such things were possible. There was a high level of personal and group dedication and integrity of purpose among us - and even so - it was a deeply miraculous experience.

It was as if we reversed the break "through spacetime," and still had the "experience," a very en-Light-ening and educational practical phenomenon, for each of us to carry forward into our lives. We taught Body Electronics groups for several years thereafter, with miraculous healings a relatively common occurrence.

A few years later Teddi was on a "wheatgrass cleanse" at the same institute, and with her was her 5 year old daughter Micah. They were there with dr. michael ryce, his friend and son Michael J. who was 7. One day there was a screech of tires, and a dog cried out. Micah 5 and Michael J. ran to the spot and pulled the dog out of harm's way. They held his hips which had been hit, and after a few minutes the dog jumped up and ran away. Micah and Michael J. had grown up with the idea that anything was possible. They never doubted, and just "acted as if!"

We realized over the years that it didn't take a point holding table, or even a group of people to do this type of work. It became a representative experience, that taught us how to assist ourselves and others to go "into the pain" and (guess what) - clear our unconscious content that (Vibrationally) caused the issue in the first place. This essence has carried into many areas of life, and offered foundational principles still valid today.

I (Cary) was with a partner on a wilderness river trip who blew out a shoulder in a rapid. He had heard me share these stories enough that he had a good understanding of the process. He also had excellent powers of concentration. I held points on him in the tent that night, and he went through his own inner journey "into the pain." He went into all the places the pain took him, to clear old crystalized thought-emotion, some even into a "past life." By the next day, his sling was off and he had oars in hand again navigating the rapids!

Revealed: Consciousness A Form of Matter!

Masaru Emoto, introduced amazing discoveries in the past couple of decades about how thought literally shapes water molecules, that show up as beautiful when associated with kind, Loving thoughts, and dis-integrative when exposed to Not of LOVE thought.

Water records energetic resonance and forms either coherent and beautiful or jagged, incoherent crystal patterns, based on thought held around it. His groundbreaking book, *The Hidden Messages in Water,* crosses boundaries between hard and soft science, with visible demonstrations of how thought-emotion Creates. His water crystals show resonance recorded in rivers, oceans, and even our bodies, or our "water vehicle" 75%-90% water.

Mr. Emoto reports conducting an experiment with chlorinated tap water at his office in Tokyo, when making crystals by his usual methods with just a few people placing thought around it was not working. He asked for the help of 500 people throughout Japan. On the appointed day and time, they all successfully sent positive thoughts to the water on his desk, with the message "Thank You." Mr. Emoto's observations on the results fortify understanding of how thoughts shift our World.

> As expected, the water changed and was able to form beautiful crystals. The chlorinated water from the tap had changed to pure water.
>
> How could this happen? I think you know the answer. Thoughts and words of 500 people reached the water without regard to borders of time and space.
>
> And in the very same way, the Vibration of your thought at this very moment is having a certain effect on the world. If you understand this, then you can also understand that you are already holding in your hands all the keys you need to change your Life.
>
> *Masaru Emoto*
> *The Secret Life of Water*

View images of Mr. Emoto's water crystals either online or in his books. They are a stupendous visual demonstration of how powerful we are as Observer-Creators.

RESTRUCTURING WATER WITH THOUGHT: Apply thought-emotion "signs" to filter or dispenser, such as LOVE, Peace, Compassion, Gratitude, Thank You, Joy, Dance, Play. Become aware of focusing your Attention on these thoughts whenever you notice your labels on the water. Enjoy drinking this water imbued with good thought-feelings of LOVE;

it often tastes sweeter. Relate to water, food, everything in Life, prayerfully, with Gratitude. Great for kids! Show them Emoto's water crystals online or in his books..

LESSON: This is an example of how thoughts affect Life. If an unkind comment occurs, it's a nice reference point to ask if they are making a not-pretty water crystal with their words, and they can change it, because they have a "picture" of what their energy is creating.

Neuroscientists and theoretical physicists Now reveal *Consciousness* is a form of matter! Giulio Tononi, U. of Wisconsin and Max Tegmark of MIT, differentiate Consciousness from other types of matter (solids, liquids, gases) with mathematically sound principles.

> ...we may finally have found a way of analyzing the mysterious, metaphysical realm of *consciousness* in a scientific manner. Latest breakthrough in this new field, published by Max Tegmark of MIT, postulates consciousness is actually a state of matter. "Just as there are many types of liquids, there are many types of consciousness," he says. With this new model, Tegmark says that consciousness can be described in terms of quantum mechanics and information theory, allowing us to *scientifically* tackle murky topics such as self awareness, and why we perceive the world in classical three-dimensional terms, rather than infinite objective realities offered by the many-worlds interpretation of quantum mechanics.
>
> ...consciousness results from a system that can store and retrieve vast amounts of information efficiently..."the most general substance that feels subjectively self-aware." This substance can not only store and retrieve data, but it's also indivisible and unified...

> *Sebastian Anthony, Extreme Tech*
> *Human Consciousness Is Simply a State of Matter*

Magically, our Attention on the *Field* affects Creation surrounding us. Miracles occur when we connect with Heart, *Essence* and Infinite possibilities, clearing ourselves of "old resonance." *21st Century Superhuman* lives in Quantum awareness that thoughts, words and emotions imprint in our "reality." "Reality" is not static, continuously flowing into New form around and through us. We are Self-Aware, and Live with Response-Ability.

We move into Living more from the Heart, expressing *Essence*. We dedicate habits of Thought and Action to the Greater Good; transitioning from service to Self to service for ALL! "There is no 'out there' out there." Ultimately, it is up to us: how we Think, Live, Eat and Play forms our Well-Being and our World. We enter Heaven here and Now, integrating with family, children, pets and Community of LOVE.

Modern medicine is not "all bad," neither is the modern World. Many incredible inventions and abilities will lead us to more amazing things. Synchronistically, our future survival as a species depends on harmonizing with nature, Earth Mother Gaia, Pachamama and her elementals, and the ever creative *Field* flowing from Source. Our greatest Achievements, Joy, Well-Being and Abundance arrive, as we enter *LOVE, Compassion, Gratitude, to Live from the Heart with True Authenticity, called En-Light-enment.* ♥ ♥ ♥

Epilogue

These are guideposts along the path to Awakening during this powerful *Shift of the Ages*. 21st Century Superhuman continues to be published as one complete book; and for ease of handling we have ALDO divided the book into 4 Parts. If you choose the route of the smaller books, please read all 4 as each contains essential "pieces to the puzzle" The exact same material is in the complete single book ***21st Century Superhuman Quantum Lifestyle.***

We invite you to Journey with us on YouTube and our Festy-Workshops and invite your friends. This miraculous journey of En-Light-enment means Living Authentically from the Heart, clearing ALL "Not of LOVE," to access and restore our Infinite True Design, LOVE. New perspectives Now unfolding allow us to live beyond the "norm," discovering our own Higher expression, to manifest our greatest dreams, desires and aspirations.

Always Question "Reality," and grow in Wisdom of your Heart and *Essence.* As Richard Feynman, Nobel Laureate Quantum physicist, said, *"If you thought that science was certain - well, that is just an error on your part,"* pointing out in ultimate wisdom -

The highest forms of understanding we can achieve
are laughter and human compassion.

Richard P. Feynman (1918-1988)
Albert Einstein Award, Nobel Prize in Physics

The "breadcrumb trail" in this guide is designed to share YOUR unique gifts with the World. Remember to as Leonard Orr says, *"Speak the Truth Quicker and Have More Fun Per Hour!"* Breathing and Smiling all the way...

Inlakesh - I am another yourself

Aloha, Many Blessings and Namaste

We bow to the Divine within You

See you "on the path!"

♥ *Cary and Teddi* ♥

LOVE

♥ ♥ ♥

Contributor

THEODORA SUSAN MULDER, PHD, CRA

Gifted with the ability to see Energy *Fields* at a young age, Teddi was drawn to metaphysical and holistic practices, opening doors for exploration of many dimensions on her Earth-Walk. She focuses on our "Grand Design."

Teddi's background and training: biofeedback Menninger Foundation; Spiritual Midwifery - The Farm Tennessee; Dr. Christopher Hill - Herbalism, Kirlian photography, cellular biology University of the Trees; Permaculture with Founder of Findhorn Peter Kaddy. She is an active meditator, initiated in Kriya Yoga, which was brought to the West by Parmahansa Yogananda. Initiated into shamanic realms she apprenticed with Sun Bear, Native American Medicine Man; mysteries of ancient Tibetan point holding with Dr. John Whitman Ray; and rebirthing techniques with Leonard Orr, Florida School of Massage. Teddi studied Cellular Biology with Dr. Bruce Lipton in Madison, Wisconsin. She completed two internships with Dr. D. A. Versendaal (founder of C.R.A. Contact Reflex Analysis), over eight years, for which she earned a PhD based in research of Clinical Nutrition, specializing in *Health of Women and Children*. Teddi has performed client services for over 30 years.

Mother of four and currently grandmother of eleven (last count); she is LOVED as an embodiment of the nurturing qualities of Mother Earth, and as one who represents the Deeper Science of Life, LOVE and Universal principles. Teddi often goes by her Soul Name, Nivana. She offers support for clarity and balance of each individual's lifestream, essential to our Future on Planet Earth and Beyond.

Her collaborative work with Cary over many years, producing classes, retreats, materials and manuals for Conscious Living, has these days moved into "midwifery" toward development of global communities through *Virtual Earth Village dot com* and **21st Century Superhuman**. She is dedicated to offering tools and resources of these visions, bringing forth our greater possibilities through implementing **Quantum Lifestyle** habits and wise Living practices.

Raising four children and many beautiful grandchildren has been the greatest learning curve of my Life - allowing each one to be who they are, supporting their individuality and their well being, to let their Lights shine in the World. Teddi ♥

146

Author

CARY DIANE ELLIS DD

Cary's Innate Ability to assimilate languages of Light and LOVE into practical everyday tools is like having the gentle hand of a friend on your shoulder, guiding you into greater Awareness.

Introducing transformation into mainstream culture for decades in the human potentials movement, she assisted thousands in breakthrough workshops: putting Tony Robbins on stage with Firewalking and Fear into Power in the 1980s; miraculous healing of her own broken arm in a matter of 6 hours when doctors wanted to do surgery and put in 2 pins; co-founder of Dolphin Camp she entered transcendental states while swimming with wild dolphins; has experienced age reversal and rejuvenation with wheatgrass, living foods and more.

Cary's wealth of knowledge comes from hands on experience as: Co-Director Hippocrates Health Institute (later Creative Health), with Lifestyle learning programs filled to capacity, exceptional organic gardens, permaculture, wheatgrass and living foods. She was Educator with Gerson Cancer Therapy Institute in Mexico, did rounds with Charlotte Gerson, experiencing "miraculous recoveries" firsthand. She trained with Dr. John Whitman Ray in revolutionary Health and Human Mind and Body Electronics and Iridology. She is also well versed in Human Design and Astrology.

Passion for the outdoors lead Cary to live remotely in high mountains of the American West, with many years of outdoor adventure, snowboarding, mountain biking, river rafting, hiking and horseback riding with her dogs and a large outdoor community. She also assisted with colloquiums for Earth-friendly building. Her lifework has been dedicated to user-friendly knowledge, easily applied to harmonious, Earth-friendly Living.

Curiosity and a sense of adventure inspired Cary to venture into unknown territories for knowledge useful, practical and necessary in our Evolutionary Leap toward a wise, ecological future. Her innate vision of Higher Dimensions, offers Light and LOVE on the Path for those seeking Wisdom for Humanity's current Evolutionary Leap. Honored for her Life-work as a Doctor of Divinity by the *Church of Tzaddi,* Cary is involved in developing cutting edge "New Earth" Communities, and is often called by her Soul Name, Kirastar.

With their current project VirtualEarthVillage.com, Cary and Teddi offer cutting edge tools to align with millions Now around the Planet ushering in communities founded in LOVE, amplifying this Current Evolutionary Wave on Planet Earth called the Shift of the Ages. ♥

Front Cover Art

FRANZI TALLEY - FRONT COVER - Earth Mother Gaia aligns with the resonance of Oneness and Harmonious living on Planet Earth, brought forth in the Ninth Wave of the Mayan Calendar, as humanity rides this wave into their own transformation through LOVE.

FRANZI TALLEY

I came from a family where creativity was always encouraged and I was, more often than not, surrounded by the sounds of classical music and a feeling of great freedom. Our neighborhood, in Bienne, a small town in the north of Switzerland. perched on the side of a deep green forest. The woods called to me daily and I answered that call.

I spent much of my time in nature, in the abundant beauty and wilderness of my country. There, I was able to ignore the over-clean, controlled, organized side of my homeland's culture. As a child I made sure to take ample advantage of delicious goods offered by numerous bakeries dotting towns, and colorful harvests in the open-air markets.

At sixteen, I began a four-year graphic design program. A few years later I moved to the US, met my husband and started a family. For the next twenty-four years we raised our children happily in Asheville, NC, as my husband worked to establish Natural Food stores all over North Carolina. During that time I was an illustrator and graphic designer for numerous projects in the Natural Foods industry. As my free time increased with the maturing of our children, I have been able to bring forth ideas and projects, carried deep inside of me for many years.

As a child I had been touched by the glory of nature and by the medieval towns of Europe with their small churches and cloisters. Their stone walls were alive with ancient art, simple and yet full of meaning. Those walls carried many stories as did the trees and the old mountain trails. The forests, lakes and valleys held within the booming mountains, are for me some of the most holy places in Creation. I have carried all of them, deep in my mind and heart for a Lifetime and to this day they provide a fertile reservoir of ideas for my work. I draw for my own enjoyment, and in the hope that my offerings will surprise, delight, amuse, and uplift others. ♥ *Franzi* ♥

NOTE: Earth Mother Gaia image on cover of this book, brought forth by artist, Franzi Talley, is aligned with the resonance of Oneness and Harmonious living on Planet Earth, and our return to LOVE activated by our transit throught the Cosmos with the Ninth Wave of the Mayan Calendar. ♥

Back Cover Art

*ENDRE BALOGH - BACK COVER - Sacred Geometry aligns with the resonance of Oneness and fractals of Creation, as we **Arc the Hologram** to transform our World with our True Design LOVE.*

ENDRE BALOGH - Violinist, Photographer, Artist

Endre's interest in spirituality has led him to Create hundreds of "Sacred Geometry" designs, the basis for his contribution to this book. Endre's extraordinary visionary work in the realms of Sound, Light and Color bring transformation to his audiences.

He is an internationally acclaimed concert violinist and soloist, who has performed for over thirty years with renowned orchestras, conductors, chamber music and productions internationally throughout Europe, Canada and the US. ***"We were under the spell of a formidably brilliant artist."*** (London Times) *"Poise and assurance, technical precision, tonal refinement and personal charm."* (new York Times) *"Dazzling technique and great gusts of temperament...eloquent master of his instrument."* (Los Angeles Times)

In 2004, curtailing his concert schedule to spend more time with his children, Endre honed his passion for photography and design. He won top awards in contests with unique aesthetic vision that earned him an enviable reputation among photographic colleagues. His photos are displayed in the collections of connoisseurs of fine photographic arts, and he has had prominent gallery showings. His photo "Egg On Glass" was chosen from nearly 3000 entries from 40 countries displayed with 87 others in the prestigious "Art of Digital" International Exhibition 2007. Endre is a highly sought after headshot photographer and graphic artist, having designed covers for numerous books. *Shutterbug* Magazine's annual publication "Expert Photo Techniques Guide" showcased his article with his cover shot and six more images inside. He was "Photographer Of the Year - 2012."

Endre's diverse work can be seen and purchased in many formats EndreBalogh.ArtistWebsites dot com Main website: EndresPhotos dot com

THANKS TO BRANDON LAVERGNE anime & manga artist, for Mediation Drawings. He can be found on Facebook as Brandon Indigo Starseed.

Bibliography

PART 4: BODY - Rejuvenation & Growing Younger with Healthy Eating, Cleanse & Detox
SECTION 1 - BACK TO THE GARDEN
Darksunblade, Review at amazon.com *Survival Into The 21st Century*
Viktoras Kulvinskas, *Survival Into The 21st Century - Planetary Healers Manual* (Omangod Press, PO Box 255, Wethersfield, CT 06109

Chapter 1 - Choosing Your Approach to Wellness
John Robbins, The Food Revolution: How Your Diet Can Help Save Your Life and Our World, (Kindle, Conari Press 2010)

Chapter 2 How Thought Affects the Body
Marco Torres, Scientist Finally Present Evidence On Expanding DNA Strands, http://preventdisease.com/news/13/012313_Scientists-Present-Evidence-on-Expanding-DNA-Strands.shtml

Chapter 3 What Is Ideal Nutrition
Dr. Caldwell Esselstyn, Prevent and Reverse Heart Dis-Ease (Avery Trade; January 31, 2008) 4-5, 84, 38
John Robbins, *Diet for a New America* (quotes online)
John Robbins, *Diet for a New World* (AVON BOOKS, A Division of The Hearst Corporation, 1350 Avenue of the Americas, New York, NY 10019 Copyright John Robbins and Jia Patton 1992) 27-28

Chapter 4 Superior Supplements: Superfoods
John D. Haymaker & Donald Weaver, The Survival Of Civilization: Carbon Dioxide, Investment Money, Population – Three Problems Threatening Our Existence http://remineralize.ning.com/profiles/blogs/hello-and-update-from-don-weaver-co-author-of-the-survival-of
Kailash Kokopelli *Walking Tree* "trust in the song of your heart" (INNER World MUSIC) Sing-dance along: http://www.kailash-kokopelli.com/songdances_kk.html   www.kailash-kokopelli.com

SECTION 2 - HOW TO CLEANSE & DETOX
Chapter 6 "7 Days" To A New YOU!
Interview by Diane with Drunvalo Melchizdek, By Enoch Tan, new Earth Daily #1 Source for Positive News

Chapter 7 Cleanse And Detox - 3-7-30 Day Cleanses
drpielet.com/3-things-you-can-do-today-to-start-losing-weight/

Chapter 9 Supportive Modalities
NAET, naet.com

SECTION 3 - DIS-EASE THE ILLUSION
Chapter 10 Toxemia The Cause of Dis-Ease
Kiera Butler, Mother Jones, *The Scary Truth About Antibiotic Overprescription* (motherjones.com/blue-marble/2013/10/scary-truth-about-antibiotic-overprescription)

Chapter 11 The Curse Causeless Shall Not Come
A Course In Miracles, Electronic Version, Chapter 2 (Copyright© 1975,1985,1992,1996 by the Foundation for Inner Peace) 16-17
Wes Annac, Aquarius Paradigm, DL Zeta: Upgrading our Lens of Perception Shifts us to Fifth-Dimensional Timelines (aquariusparadigm.com/2013/10/12/dl-zeta-upgrading-our-lens-of-perception-shifts-us-to-fifth-dimensional-timelines/ Oct. 12, 2013,)

Chapter 12 Enviro Toxins
HSPH - Harvard School of Public Health News, Impact of fluoride on neurological development in children http://www.hsph.harvard.edu/news/features/fluoride-childrens-health-grandjean-choi/
Global Healing Center's blog, Natural Health and Organic Living, Chlorine, Cancer and Heart Disease http://www.globalhealingcenter.com/natural-health/toxic-chemical-health-dangers-chlorine/

Chapter 13 Miraculous Tales
Deepak Chopra M, The Way of the Wizard: Twenty Spiritual Lessons for Creating the Life You Want (Kindle, Harmony, Random House 2009)
Edward Bach M.D. and F.J. Wheeler M.D., *The Bach Flower Remedies* (Keats Publishing Inc. New Canaan Connecticut www.keats.com 1977 The Edward Bach Center) 40-41
Energy Scientists and Developer of Vogel Crystals www.treeofLifetech.com on Dr. Marcel Vogel
Masaru Emoto, The Secret Life of Water (Kindle, Atria Books, Simon and Schuster Inc. Digital Sales 2009)
Extreme Tech, *Human consciousness is simply a state of matter, like a solid or liquid – but quantum* http://www.extremetech.com/extreme/181284-human-consciousness-is-simply-a-state-of-matter-like-a-solid-or-liquid-but-quantum

Useful Resources

Activate your DNA, put **21st Century Superhuman Quantum Lifestyle** tips and tools to work in your Life and accelerate your progress. Your personal Awakening affects the entire hologram. Express your Life with greater authenticity, empowerment and LOVE. Shift yourself. Shift the entire Hologram! *Arc the Hologram Now with LOVE!*

Keep posted at our website for more books, tools, playshops, retreats, gatherings.

If this book is in your hands, there is a special reason. It is a tool for one of the most powerful activations in human history, as we enter an Evolutionary Leap called by many *The Shift of the Ages.* This is an amazing moment in which to be participating! See You there!

SUGGESTED READING - VIEWING

Dieter Broers - *Solar Revolution*

Gregg Braden - *The Divine Matrix*

Michael Tellinger - *Slave Species of the Gods*

Graham Hancock - *Fingerprints of the Gods*

Nassim Haramein - *Youtube and theresonanceproject.org*

Bruce Lipton and Steve Bhaerman - *Spontaneous Evolution*

dr. michael ryce - *http://www.whyagain.org*

Ervin Laszlo - *New Thinking ervinlaszlo.com*

HeartMath.org HeartMath.com - *Heart Coherence Practices*

Ram Dass • Foster Gamble • David Wilcock • i-uv.com

Lynn McTaggart - *The Field and The Intention Experiment*

Sacred Sounds - Mirabai Ceiba • Deva Premal • Krishna Das
Rainbow Didge • Kailash Kokopelli

Where To Find Us

21st Century Superhuman
Quantum Lifestyle

by Cary Ellis with Theodora Mulder PhD

Amazon

Kindle

Nook

iBooks

Audio

more

Follow Us - and Share with Friends
Facebook - *21t Century Superhuman*
Youtube - *21st Century Superhuman*
Twitter.com / caryellis

www.21stcenturysuperhuman.com

~ All in progress - thank you for your patience ~
If you have skills to offer let us know - web, promo, admin
Contact us at our website or message us at Facebook.
~ *Thank you!* ~

A Virtual Earth Village Publication
VirtualEarthVillage dot com

VOLUME DISCOUNTS *check our website for details*